Never Having to Say:
Could Have, Should Have, Would Have

Roslynne Steinberg

To my friend Treva,
Best Wishes
always!
Love,
Roslynne

WALDENHOUSE PUBLISHERS, INC.
WALDEN, TENNESSEE

ISBN: 978-1-935186-66-3
Library of Congress Control Number: 2016901798
Published by Waldenhouse Publishers, Inc.
100 Clegg Street, Signal Mountain, Tennessee 37377 USA
888-222-8228   www.waldenhouse.com
Cover painting of the author by Michael Holsomback
Editing, design and type by Karen Paul Stone
Printed in the United States of America
    Native of the Jewish Bronx in New York, now a successful artist
    in Chattanooga, Tennessee, recounts overcoming her father's
    rejection and blame for the mental illness of her mother, and
    also tells of coping with the death of her own child. Includes 48
    photographs and 22 original full color paintings. -- Provided by
    Publisher
BIO026000 Biography & Autobiography: Personal Memoirs
BIO001000 Biography & Autobiography: Artists, Architects, Photographers
HIS036060 History: United States - 20th Century

Roslynne at 1320 Manor Avenue, the Bronx, New York, about 1935-36

"You can take the girl out of the Bronx,
but you'll never take the Bronx out of this girl!"
Roslynne Steinberg

Acknowledgments

This book was made possible because of my publisher, Karen Stone and my mentor, Professor Michael Holsomback. I am indeed a fortunate woman!

I am truly grateful to all those who provided me with comments, corrections, suggestions and encouragement, including: Carla Czybora, Betty Hamilton, Mitzi Elkins, Patty Maroney, Martha Owens, Kay Shore, Rosalyn Spiegel, and Treva Turner.

Contents

Preface

New York, New York! The Bronx is the northernmost of the five boroughs of New York City, in the state of New York. It was the last incorporated county of New York State. The Bronx is only forty-two square miles. Filled with iconic landmarks like the Bronx Zoo, Yankee Stadium, Pelham Bay Park, Orchard Beach, Soundview Park and so much more, there was always something to do. Many well-known people came from the Bronx, among them, Red Buttons, Dion, Geraldine Ferraro, Regis Philbin and Colin Powell.

My future unfolded where I was born in the Bronx in 1933. Filled with mostly Jewish immigrants, the Bronx was always brimming over with activity and people. We lived in the primarily Orthodox Soundview section. Street games like stickball, handball, hopscotch and potzie filled my youth. As a teenager, there were neighborhood gangs, greasers, and social clubs.

Our roots run deep. Mine are tied to family, friends and neighbors, and the sounds, sights and smells of the Bronx where I spent more than half my life. Jewish immigrants, the sweet smell of *challah* bread and the traditions of shopping at the mom and pop stores for kosher meats and egg creams are all part of my history growing up in the Bronx. The sound of Yiddish, my first language, is woven into the fabric of who I am. Saturday *Shabbat* and carp swimming in the bathtub, soon to be transformed into gefilte fish, is just one of my favorite memories of the Bronx.

Subways, trains and trolleys, such an iconic part of New York, were part of my everyday life. The Third Avenue EL, the Grand Concourse, Jerome Avenue, Fordham Road, Pelham Parkway and Tremont Avenue were my thoroughfares to adventure. It took *chutzpah*, ambition, imagination and a fierce desire to survive to navigate the streets of the Bronx. Miles of high-rise apartment buildings, blocks of tenements housing, multi-unit homes, kosher shops and deli's, Art Deco buildings and street vendors hawking their wares on every street corner were the backdrops of my life. I know you can take the girl out of the Bronx, but you'll never take the Bronx out of this girl.

Roslynne Charlotte Jacobs Steinberg
January 2, 1933

I was the first and only child of Sarah Beresofsky and Jankel Jakubavitz (Jacobs). My mother threw herself out of the hospital window shortly after I was born. She broke both of her legs. According to hospital records, the next day she was committed to the psychiatric division of Bellevue State Hospital as "an alleged insane person."

Needless to say, my father was distraught. After my unfortunate arrival into the world, any semblance of a normal home life with my mother and father was irretrievably broken. Not only did I suffer the loss of my mother, but my father also blamed me for her circumstances.

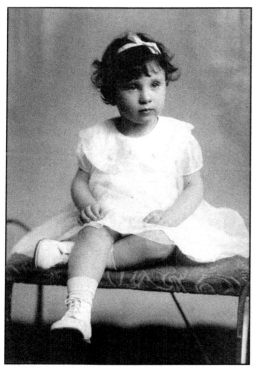

My father's parents, Elya (Alex in English) and Dora Jacobs took me to their home and raised me as their own. This ill-fated beginning has had long-lasting effects on my life.

Whether it be fate or life unfolding as God intended, let me back up and

Roslynne Charlotte Jacobs, age 2. Photo taken near the time of the wedding of her uncle Abraham to Jean Goldstein in 1935 tell you what I know about my history and tell you how this situation came to be.

Poland to America

Alex and Dora were first-generation Jewish immigrants from Poland who kept their home kosher and spoke Yiddish. They changed their name from Jakubavitz to Jacobs when they immigrated to the United States from Poland in the early 1900s. As waves of immigrants flooded the United States, it was not uncommon to Americanize foreign names. Jews have always had a challenging history, no matter the time or part of the world from where they came. Poland and Russia had been at war on and off since the tenth century. Poland, at one time, was known as a "Paradise for the Jews." Some sources say about three-quarters of all Jews worldwide lived in Poland by the middle of the 16th century.

As I understand it, my paternal ancestors lived in a *shtetl* (small village) in Eastern Europe. The early laws in the ever-changing political landscape of Poland forced Jews to live in designated quarters or ghettos. My grandparents were confined to the ghetto. Their life was challenging, becoming worse by the day; hopes for a positive future and freedom were fading. Jews were barred from many occupations in Poland. Grandfather Elya had become a tinsmith, an allowable trade. As their very existence became more difficult in the ghetto and across the region, and as the pogroms increased, a great flood of the Jewish population came to the United States.

Grandfather, Elya (Alex) Jakubavitz, also spelled Jakubo-wicz, came to the United States in 1913, from Skierniewice, a town in central Poland in Lodz province. His brother-in-law, Louis Lenchner traveled with him. He had an older brother, Altah, already in the United States, but I don't know when he immigrated.

Established before 1217, Skierniewice achieved township status in the mid-1400s. Skierniewice's most notable resident was the great composer Fryderyk Franciszek Chopin when Skierniewice was known as the Duchy of Warsaw. It was a beautiful city with many historic buildings and gorgeous architecture. The famous railway station, once part of the historic Warsaw-Vienna Railway, is still there. Many of its oldest, grand historic buildings were destroyed during the First World War.

Grandmother Dora told me that the Russians had begun drafting the Poles to build an army. She said they came into the ghetto and forced the men and older boys to line up, and every other one was conscripted to an unknown fate. The family made the decision to flee. To build a new life in a new world beyond anything they could imagine was far better than the future they saw ahead of them in Poland.

At this time, they had no idea that Hitler and his Nazi German death factories would establish extermination camps including Auschwitz-Birkenau, Belzec, Chelmno, Majdanek, Sobibor and Treblinka across Poland. Added to this evil were the concentration camps, labor camps and POW camps where countless men, women, and children died. There were three million Polish-Jewish Holocaust victims. As fate would have it, my ancestors mentioned in this story were not among them.

Fortunately, Grandpa's trade as a tinsmith served him well. Shortly after arriving in the United States and moving to the Bronx in New York, he was able to find work as a sign maker creating some of the first signs erected in Times Square. The newly named Times Square would become famous for its signs.

Grandma followed soon after, with their three children, on June 7, 1913. She brought Jacob, (my father) Abraham and Lillie with her. Jacob was six years old; Abraham was four and Lillie was just a baby. Grandma's sister-in-law, Devora, Louis

Abraham and Jankle (Jacob) Jakubavitz
came from Poland as children

Lenchner's wife, traveled with them as well as Grandpa's sisters and their children.

They boarded a ship, the *Finland,* from Antwerp, Belgium. According to the National Archives, at Philadelphia, the *Finland* was part of the Red Star Line, an international shipping line, founded in Philadelphia in 1871, as a joint venture between Americans and Belgians. The Red Star Line had ports in Antwerp, Liverpool, Southampton, New York City and Philadelphia. The line that sailed from Philadelphia to Antwerp, Belgium played a significant role in Jewish immigration to the United States from Eastern Europe.

My grandparents were poor and like all immigrants, they traveled on the steerage deck, the cheapest transportation option. My father remembers standing on the deck with his younger brother Abraham as someone from the upper deck waved to them and lowered a banana by a piece of fishing line. It was quite a novelty! Neither of them had ever seen a banana and was not quite sure it was meant to eat.

Each passenger received a ticket that read: Inspection Card - Immigrants and Steerage Passengers. Every immigrant was checked by the ship's surgeon or agent prior to or after embarkation for contagious diseases and vaccinations were required for all. The back of the card read, "Keep this Card to avoid detention at Quarantine and on Railroads in the United States." Unfortunately, Lillie was found to have diphtheria; it is an extremely infectious disease spread by direct physical contact or airborne by infected individuals. She was quarantined and had to stay on Ellis Island until she recovered. A vaccine was being developed, but not yet available. I don't know if Lillie ever recovered, because she had some abnormalities as she grew up, or maybe her issues had another cause.

I don't know much about my mother's side of the family. Her father, a Beresofsky, emigrated from Russia to London where his trade was a tailor, another allowable trade for Jews from the ghetto. Later they moved to Canada for a time. From there they went to Harlem, a neighborhood in Manhatten known as Jewish Harlem at that time, since most immigrating Jews moved there first. Eventually, many Jews migrated to the boroughs of Brooklyn and the Bronx.

The Bronx is where my father, Jankel Jacobs (changed from Jakubavitz), met my mother, Sarah Beresofsky, when they were in high school. My mother's family later changed their name from Beresofsky to Beresford. My father's name was Americanized to Jacob "Jack" Jacobs

Mother and Father

Mother was beautiful. She was petite and playful with a lovely figure. She wore her hair in a pixie cut, which accentuated her eyes and her broad smile. Known for being intelligent and well-spoken, there was no sign of mental illness when she was young, in high-school or when she was a newly-wed. It seems whatever happened to her, happened after my birth. By association, I became the cause of her illness and was blamed for her descent into madness. Maybe acceptance by my father and other adults was just too painful to bear. When Mother was carrying me, two of her sisters were consigned to mental institutions.

The Beresovskys had eight children, three boys, and five girls. Their oldest son, Ike, remained in London. Two of their daughters were already in mental asylums; no one ever spoke about the cause; we just knew it brought great shame on the family, and it was kept secret. In those days, mental institutions were known as insane asylums, a place for lunatics and called "snake pits." Mother may have suffered from schizophrenia (although this was never officially diagnosed) and not widely recognized as a mental illness, and there were no psychotropic drugs for the

My mother, Sarah Beresofsky, and father, Jankel "Jack" Jacobs, as a young couple

Mother and Father before evidence of her mental illness displayed itself

treatment of patients. Two of Mother's sisters had been subjected to electroshock treatment and prefrontal lobotomies. I met my mother's sisters, my aunts Hilda and Lillie, and they seemed very well adjusted. The boys, my uncles, Max, and Harry, appeared normal.

Sadly, my father rejected me from the time I was born. He blamed me for Mother's mental illness and had no hesitation about putting me into an orphanage. Throughout my life, I heard, "If I knew what was going to happen, I never would have had you."

Thankfully his mother, my Grandma Dora, would not hear of sending me to an orphanage. She took me home, and I became the sixth of their five children. I always called them Mama and Papa, just like the other children. 1320 Manor Avenue, the Bronx, would be my home for the next thirty-two years.

1320 Manor Avenue

Mama Dora was one tough woman! She was strong and stocky with thick hands and fingers worn from years of use; her full wavy hair was kept short and her well-worn quilted apron was part of her daily uniform. She had a strong European accent and spoke more Yiddish than English. Combined with the accent of the Bronx and a heaping dose of attitude, no one wanted to cross Mama. With a great deal of drama, she repeatedly told me, "You are my *eynikl* (first grandchild), and I would never let my *eynikl* be put in an orphanage! It would be a *shandeh* (sin)!"

My father was her favorite child, maybe because he was the firstborn. She always referred to him as, "My Jankel." I dearly loved Mama, but she had her ideas about how the world should be. She was forever in a foul mood, and she wore a wet rag around her head with an unending complaint about having constant headaches. Whoever she took a dislike to, for one reason or another, she would rant and rave and refer to them as "the gorillas." It was best not to get on the bad side of Mama!

Mama was a wonderful cook, but an atrocious housekeeper. When I arrived, most unexpectedly, they already had a full house. Mama and Papa Jacobs had three daughters, my aunts, Mae, who was twenty, Tess, fourteen and Lillie, who was twenty-three still living at home. They always referred to Lillie as "slow." Abe was going to college, but he also lived at home. Mama took me into the bedroom and laid me on the bed. The girls came in, and as usual, tossed their heavy winter coats on the bed. Mama asked, "Did you see 'vhats' on the bed? Go see 'vhats' on the bed!" When they said nothing, she leaped up and shrieked, "Oh my Gawd!" At just a few days old, I had been nearly smothered to death by a pile of thick winter coats! It seemed from the beginning my life was destined to be a struggle for survival.

Papa Alex was a gentle and sociable man. He was tall and thin as if he never filled out from the youthful slenderness of a teenager. His face was lined and weathered. His fingers were bent and gnarled, one mangled and black and blue at the tip from an accident. Life as a metal smith with rudimentary tools was challenging. Papa never complained; in very broken English, he greeted everyone with kindness.

The Bronx was considered the "Jewish Borough". At its peak in 1930 it was forty-nine percent Jewish. Our house on Manor Avenue was a typical four-family house in the Soundview section of the Southeast Bronx. We lived in the upstairs apartment, and Mama and Papa rented out the other three apartments.

Row upon row of semi-detached houses filled the street, each just a few feet apart with narrow alleyways in-between and small outdoor areas in the back. The houses were later known as row houses with "railroad apartments" as rooms were connected to each other with no separate hallway within the apartment. The hallway was on the outside of the apartment running from end to end of the building, between the entrance and the exit, in the building's common space. We lived to the left of the common hall, and another family lived on the right. Our apartment had five rooms, four in the main section and a small room over the hallway where my father slept. Mama and Papa bought the house brand new, although I have no idea where they got the money. We were fortunate to have a telephone. It was a party line, Tivoli 22248. If we needed to make a call and someone else was on the line, we had to hang up and wait our turn.

I don't remember much about Mother or my very early life until I was about three or four years old. When I was about three, I remember Mother coming to see me, along with her

The Jacobs family. Standing: Jean, Papa Alex, Mama Dora, and Mae. In front, Roslynne and her father.

sisters, Lillie, and Hilda. She gave me a bath, and I still remember the feeling of the water as it trickled down my back. When Mother and Dad married they had an apartment on East 172 Street in the Bronx, which I suppose would have become my home. It was just up the block from Mama and Papa. Mother lived in that house until her psychotic episodes forced her to go back to her parents.

Mother's psychotic episodes became more frequent. I was three or four years old and safe at Mama and Papa's house on Manor Avenue. In the dead of night, we heard a loud crash, followed by a smashing sound and wild racket in front of the house. Dad's rumble seat car was parked out front. Someone quickly shut the lights off as we peeked out of the upstairs window; Mother was smashing out all the car windows, enraged and ranting. The police arrived. When they found a knife in her purse, she screamed, "I am going to spill blood in this house!"

I don't know what happened when Mother left Bellevue, or how long she was there. Her family was living in a tenement house in Seabury place in the Bronx, about three miles from Mama and Papa. Soon after she came home from Bellevue, her family bought a small farm in New Berlin, New York. It was in both Mother's and her father's name. I don't know if my father helped buy the farm in the hope the wife he knew would return. They needed a place she could be away from people, a place that might heal her mental illness and save her from life in an insane asylum. In those days, asylums were a death penalty. If your body survived shock treatments and a lobotomy, your brain was left in a dysfunctional state, and you remained institutionalized for life.

I discovered a letter Mother had written to my Uncle, Abe. She referred to the farm as the "olde shacke" and she asked about me. I must have been very young because she asked Uncle Abe if I had any more teeth sprouting. She said she was feeling rather restless and aching to go home. She also said she and Jack had been apart, and she was longing to go home to see him, which must have been at the apartment on East 172 Street. It seems my father had put all the furniture in storage, so maybe he had decided the marriage was not going to work. In the state of New York, the law did not allow someone to divorce a mentally ill person.

Time Moves On

As time went on, Mother faded into the tenements of Seabury place, and I seldom saw her. Family, neighborhood friends and play filled my home life. I had a feisty, fiery and funny personality, which was how I was able to entertain myself at home. I was my own best audience. The adults were usually busy, and Mama Dora stayed mired in chores. Papa Alex left the house early. He was exhausted at day's end after a long day of hard physical labor. My father was seldom home, and when he was, he ignored me. I sat on the stoop on Sunday afternoons when the street was nearly empty, with an aching sadness tearing at my heart, knowing my friends were with their families and out with their fathers. I would catch myself glancing to the right and to the left, somehow believing that he would appear. I too wanted a story to tell about the fun weekend with my family at school the next week. I never did.

I was ready for kindergarten, but Yiddish was the only language I spoke, and English was required. Mama begged the school to take me, and they finally agreed. I was four and a half and in many ways I felt like this is where my life began. I finally had friends my age to play with, and I was stepping into my personality. The first day of school Tess proudly sent me off with my hair in banana curls tied with bows.

The neighborhood was always a grand adventure offering an exciting variety of sights and sounds. Hundreds of people lived on our block in high-rises, row-houses, and apartments. The community was bursting with activity, from kids playing games in the street, to women stopping to chat as they carried in their shopping. Workers bustled through the streets to hawk their wares and supply daily deliveries. Of course, there was no air-conditioning, and with cramped quarters, everyone spent as much time as possible outside, especially the kids.

I learned to be clever and resourceful and to entertain myself. Life was fascinating from my perspective. Just sitting on the stoop I could be endlessly amused by the passersby. Life was a colorful, never ending stream of activity, from the neighbors that Mama called Communist, who, as she declared, all believed in free love, to the many delivery people busy shuttling coal, cases of seltzer and bottles of milk.

The Great Depression had affected the entire nation and beggars on the tramp emerged from the alleyways calling out, "I cash clothes; I cash clothes." As gruff as Mama could be when a beggar came to the door asking for food, she never hesitated to go to the kitchen and make a sandwich. In the evenings, after supper, the streets were filled with people coming together to chat, relax and take a break from a hard day's work.

James Monroe High School was directly across the street from our house on Manor Avenue. The back of the school, a two-story concrete wall filled with pockmarks and rat holes, towered above a long row of weathered green benches that lined the sidewalk. This concrete wall served as the social hub of our block. Gasoline was rationed, and very few of our neighbors owned a car, so traffic was never an issue. It seemed everyone knew everyone else in the neighborhood and their business. Young lovers sat on the stoops or benches, and women gathered to catch up on neighborhood news. Men came to smoke and talk politics. Beggars came looking for food, cigarette butts and discarded bottles to cash in.

Children ran in the streets weaving their way through the many vendors with pushcarts hawking "jelly apples", apples on a stick dipped in a pot of molten red jelly. If you couldn't afford a nickel for an apple, you could buy a jellied marshmallow for a couple of pennies. There were carts filled with hot sweet potatoes and carts filled with fried food and baked delights. All of the kids loved the candy cart pushed by Sam; the Candy

Man. Sam was a pint-sized old man with a head full of unruly white hair and a long white mustache. He patiently filled orders as giggling, wide-eyed, eager children lined up with their pennies. The best treat of all was when Jimmie the Greek arrived with the Bungalow Bar, a little white ice-cream truck with a brick roof on top. His hand thrust from the window clanging a large brass bell as he called out, "Ices, cups, fudge bars!" Creamsicles, ice-cream sandwiches and every imaginable pleasure hidden behind the walls of the Bungalow Bar brought a swarming mass of kids clutching nickels and dimes in sweaty palms.

Some of the ice-cream bars had a special "lucky stick" that entitled you to free ice-cream. I would get up at six o'clock in the morning to scour the streets and under the benches to search for lucky sticks, knowing that the lovers' minds were on things other than a free ice-cream. Timing was critical. As the dawn was breaking, huge rats the size of cats would scurry back into the holes in the wall. Watching from the upstairs window as the last of their long tails slithered into the recesses of the wall, I ran out to collect the lucky sticks before the street sweepers came. I usually gathered enough to keep me in free ice-cream for the week.

My school, PS (Public School) 77 was diagonally across the street from our house. I couldn't wait to see what was happening behind the doors of that school. I was so excited to be there, but I had seldom heard English spoken. At that time, classes were ordered from first grade through eighth-grade and each class was divided into A and B segments. Mama was not able to help me with school work. Occasionally Aunt Tess helped me, but she was living the busy life of a high school student.

I quickly realized I was on my own and school was tough! Mrs. Guerra, my teacher in 1A, helped me make it through the first half of the year. Ms. Downey, my 1B teacher, took an instant dislike to me. I did something to make her mad. I don't remember what it was, but I will never forget the slap across my face and the sting it left on my cheek and the shame I felt in my heart. Held back, I had to repeat 1B. This time around, I was top banana. I was learning English and making friends. When I was invited to the homes of my friends, it dawned on me how poor we were and how filthy our house was. Mama Dora was a pack rat, and our house was a perpetual mess.

I am so grateful for Ms. Koslin, my third-grade teacher because she arranged for me to go away to summer camp through the Jewish Federation program for underprivileged children. I spent two weeks on a life-changing adventure. It was the first time I had ever been away from my neighborhood. I was so proud that my new outfit wasn't a hand-me-down. I was in a cabin where all the girls were from Brooklyn, except me. The boroughs of New York have always had unique identities and competition between them. Our camp counselor asked, "Who has artistic ability?"

Excited to prove the kid from the Bronx had some talent, I eagerly said, "I do!"

A cabin mate surrounded by her pals from Brooklyn sneered, "I can draw better than you."

I shot back, "Fine, let's see."

The counselor decided the girls should judge the winner. Of course, the Brooklyn girls rallied around their hometown pal, and I got one vote, my own. I learned something about myself that day. No matter the odds, I was always going to stand-up for myself. It would be more than fifty years before I rekindled my love of creating art.

As I progressed in school, I had an opportunity that again changed my life. I was painfully skinny causing Mama Dora much concern. She feared I would become sickly. With all her worries and trash talk about the neighbors and the state of life, in general, she loved me and always tried to do her best on my behalf. I enrolled in Mrs. Karol's health improvement class for students needing extra attention. Mrs. Karol would become my guardian angel.

One big room held all the grades, 3 A&B through 8 A&B. Even though 3B, my class, was taught last, I heard everything that was taught to every grade. We learned math, English, history, geography, and art. Rest period included milk and cookies and quiet time on a fold-out cot. I walked home for lunch, which was right across the street. Mama had a pretzel egg for me, a crusty fried egg with a roll and butter. I listened to stories on the radio and headed back to school until three in the afternoon. My health and well-being began to improve.

My Aunt Tess holding me as a baby at home, 1320 Manor Avenue

Life at Home

Tess, Lillie and I shared a room together. Tess was like a mother to me, and I adored her. Because she was fourteen years older than I was, she was able to take me for walks and also be a playmate. Mama Dora had her hands full just managing the house and the chores without modern conveniences. Mama Dora spent so much time cursing the neighbors and being so spiteful she made herself miserable. Her favorite phrase for anyone that annoyed her, which was most of the neighbors, and the delivery people she thought gave poor service, was *"Gei kakn oifn yam!"* (Drop dead!)

Lillie had always been considered "slow." She would wander about muttering to herself and giggling. Mama Dora would soak her scarf in cold water and tie it around her head and mutter, *"Zol Got mir helfen!"* (May God help me!) Mama always said Lillie began doing the same *Shtiklech* (tricks) that my mother was doing, which was when they recognized something was wrong with her.

The gnawing fear that I was sure to follow hung in the air. When I was four or five years old, I was alone with Lillie in our room. She was fondling me more from curiosity than evil intent, but I could not escape, and I knew this was not right. I screamed!

Papa shoved our door open. He bellowed, *"Vas iz dos?"* ("What is this?") It was the final straw to an unmanageable situation. Lillie, who was twenty-three, was put into Pilgrim Hospital for the mentally impaired in Central Islip, New York.

Mama and Papa loved her dearly, and this was another blow to an already difficult existence. I cannot imagine how helpless they must have felt. Every weekend, no matter how exhausted they were from the week, they woke up early to make the long trip to visit Lillie. Mama made Lillie's favorite sandwiches and treats then they walked four long blocks to the Soundview Avenue station and took the train all the way to Manhattan. From there, they caught the Long Island railroad to Central Islip and Pilgrim Hospital. Lillie spent the rest of her life in an insane asylum. She had both electroshock treatment and a prefrontal lobotomy. No one ever understood what caused her mental illness and the treatments in hospitals were nothing short of barbaric in the 1930s. Mama always believed it was because of the diphtheria she had as an infant when they landed at Ellis Island.

Mae, who had disarming good looks, married Milton Luban, and they lived just down the street at 1258 Manor Avenue. I spent much time at their house because I was always warmly welcomed. Uncle Milton paid attention to me, and he was full of fun. He filled a hole in my life that my father never did. They had two children, Clifford, and Howard, for whom I babysat as I grew older.

Uncle Abe married Jean Goldstein. They also stayed in the neighborhood at 1236 Stratford Avenue. They had two children, Norman, and Carol. The Goldstein families were colorful characters. Of course, Mama Dora, in her usual state of discontent, hated the Goldstein's because they came from Latvia instead of Poland, as if they had a choice of where they were born!

My father, who was now estranged from my mother, worked for a novelty house where they made *tchotchkes* (trinkets). He was good with numbers and was an assistant bookkeeper, eventually going back to school to become the full-time bookkeeper. He moved back to Manor Avenue in his former bedroom that was a little room over the stairway. Even though he never accepted the responsibility of being a father ,Mama always endearingly referred to him as "My Jankel." He had always been her favorite. Mama spoiled him. She waited on him as though he was a prince. She always served him a huge breakfast even though he never helped with my care, and he repeatedly said, "If I had known what would happen to Sarah, I never would have had a child!"

My father lived his life as a single person, and I vaguely remember different women on his arm. He took a trip to Canada, and I was so excited because he promised to bring me something. With the anxious anticipation of a child, I could not wait to see what he had for me in his suitcase when he returned. All he said was, "I must have left it on the train."

He met a woman named Natalie, and they moved in together in a place at 2956 Bainbridge Avenue, in the west Bronx not far from the Grand Concourse. The Grand Concourse was built as a means of connecting the borough of Manhattan to the northern Bronx. It was considered the Park Avenue of the middle-class. An ordinary lifestyle was elevated to affluence just by saying you lived there.

In the state of New York, it was illegal to divorce a person who was deemed mentally ill by the court, so Father was still legally married to Mother. The only way he could get around this was to change his name for the fourth time. Born Jankel Jakubavitz, when he arrived in the United States, his name was changed to Jacob Jacobs and later Americanized to Jack Jacobs. In order to re-marry, and in the hopes my mother would not be able to track him, he changed his name once again. This time he became Jack Jamieson, a far cry from Jankel Jakubavitz.

My father and Natalie faded from my life. My last memory of them was going to their house at Christmas. They had a Christmas tree with presents underneath. When I told Mama Dora about this, because this was an unusual sight for a Jewish girl, Natalie and Father denied it! Rather than question my sanity, this time I began to hold firm to what I knew to be the truth and carefully decide what to believe from adults.

Once again, I felt myself spinning in a game of chance. The adult world and the constant life changes and oppressive energy were beyond anything I could comprehend. When I was in first grade, I had to go to court and tell the judge with whom I wanted to live, my mother or my father. Life was always in some kind of upheaval.

Mama Dora said, "You tell the judge you are going with your father!" I was terrified of my mother, and I knew I would never want to be near her. On the other hand, I didn't feel close to my father. He simply ignored me, and I had heard Mama say so often to Natalie in her loud Yiddish voice, "The vey you treat this child, God is going to punish you!" I was afraid if I chose my father I would be taken from Mama, Papa and Tess. I knew I had to do as Mama Dora told me, and thankfully when I chose my father, it just meant that he was free to leave me with Mama and Papa. He did send five dollars a month to help them with my care.

Daily Life

We celebrated *Shabbat* from sundown on Friday until sundown on Saturday. It was a day of rest. Shortly before sunset on Friday night, we would turn off the electric lights and light candles to usher in peace and blessings to our home and the world. Papa went to Synagogue on Jewish holidays, but Mama never went. At that time, only men went to the synagogue.

I loved Saturday because Papa was home. We would walk around the neighborhood and stop at the local shops filled with cultural variety and richness of sights, sounds, and smells. When we stood at the corner of East 172nd Street and Manor Avenue, just before we crossed the street, a strong wind tunnel of cold air always seemed to arise. Papa said this was once an Indian graveyard and the cold air came from the Indian people buried here, as though their messages from the grave were carried on the wind. As an adult, I can only imagine what he must have remembered from his childhood in Skierniewice and the horrors of the ghetto as he thought of the Indian graveyard.

Mama and Papa were Orthodox Jews, and our home was kept kosher. They were serious about following the dietary laws. We never ate pork or shellfish, and I can still hear Mama say, "Be careful not to mix up the *milchig* (milk) and *fleishig* (meat) utensils and dishes!" Mama was always cooking, especially for Shabbat. In the Bronx, there were small "mom and pop" shops everywhere, each with a different offering. We walked two blocks down from Manor Avenue to the EL on Westchester Avenue where all the shops were.

We always stopped at the neighborhood fish store where Mama would carefully choose a huge whitefish or carp from a glass tank to make gefilte fish. It was always live so she would let it swim in the bathtub for a couple of days until she was ready to use it. One swift whack on the head with an iron skillet and the fileting began.

Chicken soup was standard fare and we would go to the kosher chicken shop and pick a bird freshly killed by the Rabbi that morning. It cost an extra nickel to buy one plucked by a chicken flicker, so Mama usually plucked it herself and then singed it over our gas stove. Chickens were on one side of the shop and beef on the other.

Butchers only sold the front end of a cow, which was considered kosher, and it had to be eaten within three days. Mama would chat with the butcher and pick out a nice piece of brisket then barter for a fair price. Armed with sacks of brown paper, we made our way through countless street vendors selling everything from fruit to frankfurters and headed to our last stop, the appetizing store. A mouth watering variety of salads, lox, smoked whitefish and cream cheese filled the cases. We made our final purchases and headed home to fill the house with the unique smells and tastes so familiar to all Jews on Shabbat.

Mama made fresh noodles and rolled the dough so thin it was almost transparent before she cut it. Her challah bread was sweet and fragrant. *Shabbat* dinner was followed by hand-made strudel, sponge cake or spiced honey cakes that were extra moist and sweet. We drank seltzer water or hot tea in glasses with a tea ball hanging from the side to steep the tea. The seltzer was delivered every week in a wooden crate.

The dining room was huge. A long, massive table sat in the middle. Equally substantial chairs were along the sides and ends. A china cabinet sat at the end of the room, and a large sideboard lined the wall. The furniture nearly filled the room. With family and guests, it was not unusual to have twelve people at the table. Most of the time we ate in the kitchen, and the dining room was used for crowds and always for Passover.

I don't know why, but until I was about eight years old, I always ate before or after the family, but never with them. If I was in the kitchen, I usually sat under the table to eat. Shoes, skirts, and pant legs kept me occupied, and I became very resourceful at meeting my needs.

The chores were never done. When the iceman came, he would expertly wield his pick to get just the right size block for our icebox. We were charged by the weight. We didn't have a washing machine, so Mama used a huge porcelain tub built into the wall, and she used a washboard to scrub our clothes. She had an old wooden ironing board with a piece of asbestos at the end where she laid the hot iron. To wet the ironing, Mama just took a big swig of water, pursed her lips and spewed on the clothes.

I can still hear her saying, "Zol Got mir helfen!" (May God help me!) as she cooked, ironed and complained about the constant headaches. Mama spent so much time being hateful and cursing other people that I often wondered if that caused her headaches.

The coal truck came once a month and dumped coal clattering down a chute into the basement. A tall black man named Charlie tended the furnace, the coal stove, and the hot water stove every morning and evening to keep our hissing and clanking radiators delivering heat to the house. Charlie was a staunch Republican, and Papa Alex was a Democrat. They would debate the politics of their party and occasionally end the debate with a little schnapps and a toast wishing each other good health.

Papa spoke broken English and loved getting the newspaper on Sunday mornings because it was written in Yiddish. It was called *The Yiddish Daily Forward* and filled with sepia pictures of local news. The paper discussed trade unionism and politics, and he was interested in both. According to

Yiddish Sources, the *Forward* came to be known as the voice of the Jewish immigrant and the conscience of the ghetto. It fought for social justice, helped generations of immigrants to enter American life and broke some of the most significant news stories of the century. It was among the nation's most eloquent defenders of democracy and Jewish rights because it was written in Yiddish.

I loved going to the candy store! I went right after school to my favorite store on the corner of Morrison Avenue and East 172 Street. Papa sent me to pick up the *Daily Forward* and his favorite, celery soda. I had a penny or two left after buying the paper and soda for Papa. With my mouth watering, I would look at the rows of jars filled with candy and buy myself a treat. Tootsie Rolls were my favorite!

The trade union was especially important to Papa. Not only did he do metal work, but he also worked on stage sets and did construction work in Manhattan. I remember the metal sign he made to advertise his business. A. Jacobs – Tin Smith and Roofing.

As the economy was still struggling to recover from the Great Depression, a job was not always easy to come by. Papa needed work, so he went to work while the union was striking. He was severely beaten and accused of being a scab (a strike-breaker) because he was willing to cross the picket lines and work while the strike was going on.

Fortunately, between 1935 and 1943, the WPA or Works Progress Administration was implemented by order of President Franklin Delano Roosevelt. It helped provide jobs for unemployed men and women to carry out public works projects for those struggling with the effects of the Great Depression. Papa was a proud man with self-respect and a strong work ethic. He didn't want to accept public assistance or "go on the dole" and he was thankful to find construction work as part of this program. Papa's resilience, hard work and hope for a better tomorrow left an indelible mark on me.

We were feeling the pinch of the Depression, but maybe not as much as many people because we were already poor and didn't have as far to fall. Mama had to cut expenses, and we lost our telephone, which had been one of our few luxuries. One of the wealthiest kids in the neighborhood, whose family owned the only car on our block, was a friend from school. I would go to her house on the corner and ask her mom to use their phone so I could call my father and beg him for a quarter, my biweekly allowance. I could go to the candy shop, or just have a few pennies of spending money.

One day her mother said to me, "Why do you come here to use our phone? Go find a nickel and use the public phone on the corner!"

She had no idea how much a nickel meant to an eight-year-old. Eventually, when I could get my father on the phone and tell him I needed my quarter, he would tell me to take the El from Soundview to East 125th Street in Harlem to meet him. Thankfully, I was so skinny and small that I didn't have to pay the turnstile toll if I could fit underneath the bar. He would give me that lousy quarter, and I would stop at the candy store on the way back home and spend a nickel on all the candy I could eat. It was enough to have a "party" and invite friends over for a treat.

Natalie and Father married when I was eight years old.

The Cast of Characters

When I was eight years old, my father married Natalie. I have no idea where they met or how long they had been together before they married. I had met her on several occasions, but never liked her, and never considered her a stepmother. Mama Dora was the only mother I ever knew.

Natalie had legs like twigs and Mama used to lament, "Look at those legs and her *mies* (ugly) *tokhes* (butt)! She looks like she has leprosy!" Natalie's legs were covered in horrible runny sores. "Vhy, oh vhy, would my Jankel want to be with her? *Oy vey iz mir!*" (Oh, woe is me!)

My aunts said, "How can he go to bed with her?" They loved me and had no idea these kinds of comments added to my feelings of rejection.

Uncle Milton overheard Dad tell Natalie that he had made an "arrangement" and she would never have to take care of "the kid." Once again, I was feeling miserable at being abandoned by my father. Shortly after Father married Natalie, they moved to Tennessee. I never heard from him and it would be years before I saw him again. By this time, I felt as if my heart would have failed if I had to bear any more rejection. I was completely numb.

Grandfather Beresofsky paid a rare visit to our house. He had a Russian, British and Bronx accent all rolled into one. With his irrepressible optimism, he was always singing, *Pack up Your Troubles in Your Old Kit-Bag, and Smile, Smile, Smile.* It was a World War I marching song published in 1915 in London. He was a tailor and he said to me, "I'm going to make you a special suit. What's your favorite color?"

Mama Dora said, "Why don't you thank him?

I suppose I was angry at anyone that had anything to do with my mother. All I could say was, "I'll thank him when he brings me the suit."

Mama Dora bragged to the rest of the family about my rude response and I felt so smart and happy that I had pleased her. Looking back, I can only imagine how difficult his life must have been having three mentally ill daughters and living in a tenement. He did make that suit in a bright green fabric, my favorite color, with a vest and skirt. I hardly wore it because I felt like anything to do with my mother was tainted.

I was a nosey kid, more as a way to entertain myself than anything else. Our house with four apartments and common hallway was a treasure trove of discovery. Much of my education about life, in general, came from the diverse group of tenants in our four-family house. It was a cast of characters thrown together by fate.

Our apartment was upstairs on the left. The Shapiros lived upstairs across the hall. You might think that Mama Dora would find a common bond with close neighbors, but with her usual distaste for people, she called Mrs. Shapiro a "Cock-eyed Jenny." She was Jewish in name only and was known as a trollop. Mr. Shapiro, a plumber, was a good looking guy. They had a daughter, Eva, who was my age, but we didn't seem to have much in common. Tess loved to spend time with Mrs. Shapiro because she always got an earful about men, loose women, and sex. It was twisted, but at eight years old I suppose this was the beginning of my sex education.

The Marmals, a family downstairs in the back, owned an appetizing store that they worked for six days a week. They were devout Orthodox Jews and Mrs. Marmal always wore a *sheitel* (wig) worn by some Orthodox married Jewish women to obey the Jewish Law of covering her hair.

The first time I met their tall, fair-haired son, I thought he was cute. Turns out, their towheaded, thirteen-year-old son had a rampant case of raging hormones. He always had a friendly smile and wanted to chat. I was thrilled to have a pal in the building at least somewhat close to my age until he tried to press me into the corner of the hallway and began groping me. Their door opened right next to the door to the basement. The basement had been a fun place to explore until they moved in.

I had overheard Tess talking about sex enough to know that feeling like this wasn't right. I welled up with shame, embarrassment and disgust every time I saw him. I had to sneak outside to avoid his leers and his friendly smile turned into an ugly intention. I would hear, "Pssst" and see him waiting for me, motioning me to come over. I would run the other direction, petrified I might get trapped in the basement with him, but also, too afraid and ashamed to tell anyone what was happening.

It has always been natural for people of the same race and religion and like values to congregate together. I had no idea that there was a bigger world outside of New York and the Bronx, where everyone I knew was Jewish, including all of the shopkeepers and most of the street vendors and neighbors.

The LaRacas, an Italian family of Catholics, lived downstairs in a four-room apartment. Mrs. LaRaca was heavy set and always wore a dreary long black dress though she was always pleasant to me. They were the only Italians and the only Catholics I had ever met, as well as the only gentile family we had ever rented to. I think this is the first time I began to realize that the world was not Jewish. Of course, Mama ranted about the LaRacas. She said they used too much hot water and always had too many people over.

Just before World War II broke out, thankfully, the Shapiro's moved out and the Hoffburgs moved in. They had a beautiful blonde baby and always welcomed me into their apartment, just across the hall. Mrs. Hoffburg, who I called Ruth, was always filled with laughter. She had a regular babysitter, Annie. Annie was Greek and so much fun! She was a neighbor just down the street at 1312 Manor Avenue. We played "Monopoly," "War" and "Go Fish," and they always had delicious treats like cookies or tapioca pudding. We had nothing social at our apartment, no laughter, and no games or toys because Mama Dora had no time for such foolishness.

World War II

I was almost nine years old when World War II broke out after the devastating attack on Pearl Harbor by the Japanese on December 7, 1941. Papa Alex was offered a job in a defense plant run by the Department of Defense in Baltimore, Maryland, as a riveter, using his metal smithing skills. Eventually, the WPA was liquidated as the nation banded together to support the war effort.

Baltimore was more than two-hundred miles from the Bronx and a long way by bus or train. Papa came home on the occasional weekend, as he was able. This experience opened up the whole new world for Papa. All he had ever known was the ghetto in Skierniewice, Poland, and life in the Bronx. When he came home, he told us stories about movies he had seen and about meeting large numbers of working *shvartz* (black) people for the first time. Money was tight and Mama always watched for his check in the mail and was grateful for the five dollars my father sent for my care.

The war permeated every aspect of our lives. We had air raid drills at school and were taught to cover our heads with our arms and roll into a ball under our desks. Everyone was issued a small round plastic disk with our name and date of birth on it that we were required to wear around our necks.

I loved hearing Papa's stories, and I wanted to be a patriot and do my fair share for the war effort. Little did I understand the devastating horror the Nazis were inflicting in Poland, and that Sobibor, a notorious death camp, was built near Skierniewice, the former home of my grandparents.

I decided my contribution would be to collect tin foil. I walked door to door through the neighborhood asking for scraps from cigarette packs. My efforts were rewarded when I was given a huge ball of foil that had been created from hundreds of small pieces. We had done without so much that I was happy to give it to Papa who said he could use it for soldering. We had always been poor, so cutting back on essential things and not wasting was not hard. Gasoline, sugar, butter and many essential supplies were rationed, but we never had a car and a lot of necessary supplies had always been luxuries for us, so it didn't affect us too much. We recycled every piece of metal we could find. Old bobby pins, broken zippers, and foil. Cans were saved in the "wash and squash system." It felt good to do something positive for the war effort.

Tess and I were the only ones left at home. Tess got a job at the main post office on West 34th Street in Manhattan posting and sorting mail. For the first time in history, the post office now employed women. Tess was at the age to think about marriage but, unfortunately, most of the eligible bachelors were 4-F, or candidates that were found to be unfit for military service and no one wanted to date them.

Growing Up

I was growing up. I had gone from a skinny kid running the streets of the Bronx and slipping under the subway turnstiles to a young teenager. The Harrod Avenue Library became my sanctuary. I was swept away by fairy tales, and I could always relate to the forlorn princesses, ever hopeful for rescue. I checked out as many books as I could carry. I was lost in an imaginary adventure on my way to and from the library, always finding an interesting shortcut. There was an enormous hill behind Stratford and Morrison to climb and countless shadowed alleys to slip in and out of, a skill I had mastered escaping from Mother.

Orchard Beach on Long Island Sound was the place to be in the summer. I hitched a ride with neighbors as hundreds descended on the beach to avoid the sweltering heat. There were food vendors, playgrounds and picnic areas. I always brought a cheese sandwich wrapped in waxed paper, and if I had a little spending money, a frozen malted was my favorite treat.

During the long, stifling hot summer days the neighborhood kids spilled into the streets. We played handball and curb ball, no bat needed; you just sent a small hard rubber ball flying against a wall or the curb. If you weren't quick, you ended up with a fat shiner when it came back and smacked you. Boys played Jonnie on a Pony and girls played hopscotch and Potzie. We all played endless games of Hide and Seek. The streets were our playground because just a few people in our neighborhood owned cars.

I worked hard to collect soda bottles, scouring the streets and alleys to turn them in for a penny apiece. Bottles were recycled, sanitized and refilled. If I scraped up a few cents, I would buy a treat or go to a movie. Along with the candy store,

Woolworths 5 and 10 on Westchester was a favorite. I loved the movies. There was always a double feature for a dime. Movies didn't come and go quickly, and we didn't have multiple theaters. When new movies arrived, I couldn't wait. The Ward Theater was between Ward and Boynton Avenues. Ida Lupino, Humphrey Bogart, Shirley Temple, Veronica Lake, Charlie Chaplin and Mikey Rooney were popular actors. The Three Stooges, Our Gang, Pinocchio and anything with Shirley Temple were some of my favorite movies.

When I was nine or ten years old, I was at a Three Stooges movie and doubled over laughing so hard that I hit my mouth on the seat in front of me. Crack! My front tooth broke in half leaving me with a snaggle-toothed smile until I was sixteen years old. No one noticed anything different at home, or if they did it was never mentioned. The only doctor or dentist I had ever seen was at school, which had always provided health care. I was told I would have to wait until I was sixteen to get my tooth replaced because they were still growing. As if adolescence wasn't difficult enough, now I had developed an awkward smile to try and cover-up my broken tooth. I was determined life would not pass me by. My personality and humor began to blossom.

Papa Alex

Near the war's end, Papa Alex came home from Maryland to stay. He was always slender, but he had gotten frightfully thin. He had a constant hacking cough and Mama Dora took him to see Dr. Adair, a cancer specialist in Manhattan. Lung cancer was the diagnosis. Mama even began cooking bacon, completely against the Jewish law, in a desperate attempt to help Papa gain weight.

I don't think I really understood how sick my dear Papa was until his health declined so much that he was bedridden. He was weak, pale and rail thin with a layer of gray flesh covering his protruding bones. I felt so helpless, but I came to a place of acceptance because I knew there was nothing I could do. On May 27, 1946, I was awakened by the cries of Mama. At just sixty years old, our beloved Papa, the only father I had ever known, was gone.

Our home became a place of mourning according to the Orthodox Jewish traditions. The rabbi came to talk to Mama. Papa's older brother, Altah, and his brother-in-law, Lenchna, became his *Shomers* (Watchmen) and stayed with Papa's body until his burial. Many men came and gathered around his bed with unceasing prayers spoken in Hebrew, little of which I understood. Papa was dressed in the traditional white burial garments by the *Chevra Kadisha*. These garments symbolized that we are all equal in death and we take nothing with us because God judges a man on our merits, not our worldly wealth. Tradition called for Jews to be buried within three days in a simple wooden casket and no flowers because they are considered a frivolous adornment.

Papa was buried at the Independent Skierniewicer Benevolent Association, a special section of Mount Moriah Cemetery in Fairview, New Jersey, founded in New York in

1913 by immigrants from Skierniewice, Poland. I too will be buried there one day and reconnected to the family that raised me and to my ancestors from Poland.

Roslynne and Mama Dora, 1945

Surviving the Summer

I was thirteen years old when Papa Alex died. Mama Dora went through a period of mourning, and Uncle Milton and Aunt Mae thought a few weeks in the country, in upstate New York for the summer, would give Mama a much-needed rest. Bungalow colonies were a popular way for people stuck in the oppressive heat of the city to escape for an inexpensive, fun, relaxing change of pace.

In fact, the Catskills were once known as the Jewish Alps or the Borscht Belt. Jewish farmers began renting rooms and cottages by the week to boarders. They became a regular summer retreat for lower-and middle-class Jews. There was a lot of community space, from vast gathering rooms and dining halls to the *kocha lien* (community kitchen) and shared bathrooms. The community kitchen had rows of small stove top burners and cupboards to store pots and pans so families would have a place to cook.

The woods and fields of the Catskills were an invitation to hike or go for a leisurely stroll. Dances, bonfires, and sing-a-longs were part of the fun. It was a time to relax and escape the burdens of everyday life. This seemed to be just what Mama Dora needed. Aunt Mae and her two boys, Clifford and Howard, along with Mama, started packing for their trip.

It was decided that I should go stay with my father and Natalie in Chattanooga, Tennessee, for two months of the summer. I hadn't seen either of them for years and was not looking forward to it. I boarded a train with a sleeping berth for an overnight trip. I didn't have much to take for the summer. Everything fit a small round patent leather suitcase with a strap on top. I was very proud of the new outfit Mama sewed for me, a purple ruffled blouse and a pair of banana yellow pants.

I was just thirteen, but I felt very glamorous in my new clothes and very mature to take a trip by myself, even with my odd snaggletoothed smile. I met a young woman who was traveling with her mother to visit her husband at Fort Bragg. We had a great conversation. I had spent so many years taking care of myself and learning how to get along with strangers that I felt very confident traveling by myself.

I changed trains in Washington, D.C., and then went on to the final stop in Tennessee. The train pulled into the Chattanooga Choo Choo, and my father met me at the station. He and Natalie lived on Cemetery Avenue near Central and Main Street on the west side of the National Cemetery. Natalie and my father went into the mom and pop grocery business; my father was the store bookkeeper. I heard somewhere he had also learned to cut meat, but I couldn't imagine him as a butcher.

Mom and pop stores dotted the landscape. That was where everyone shopped, before the days of supermarkets. Many of the mom and pop shops were in poor neighborhoods where credit was big business and extending credit to customers was typical. While I did not like a lot of things about Natalie, I thought she was a hard worker, and my father needed a strong woman in his life.

Natalie and my father never had children, and I could not help but remember when Mama Dora cursed Natalie so long ago. She was defending me, saying, "The way you treat this child, you will never have children of your own! God will punish you!" At some point, Natalie was pregnant and miscarried. I always felt like Mama's curse had come true to punish her. So many years had passed, yet I still felt as though I was that young child who was an unwelcome burden in their lives.

I spent most of the time alone around the house. I sat on the porch and read, or I chatted with their next door neighbors, none of whom was my age. I had been there a few days when Natalie told me to clean out the dog pens, a nasty, disgusting job. It was evident that I was no more than Cinderella to her. It was the first time I ever heard my father stand up for me. He said, "No, she will not clean out the pens."

Natalie was furious. For the rest of my short visit, all that she would say to me was, "Go ask your father!" I was trying to iron a blouse like I did at home, using a blanket on a chair, and I accidently burned her chair. I tried every way possible to fix it, but nothing made any difference. Natalie had all she could stand of me after one short week and I was utterly miserable. I could not believe this was summer vacation.

I was sent away to spend the rest of the summer on Lookout Mountain with Natalie's brother Ike and his family. I met her oldest nephew, Harold, and we had a teenage summer fling of stolen kisses, something that finally felt good, after the miserable vacation I had suffered through. The family was nice enough, but by the end of my second week in Tennessee I was ready to go home.

My father came to pick me up, and I was sent back to the Bronx by train with a pile of ill-fitting, unfashionable castoffs. Mama Dora was so upset and called the clothes *schmattas* (rags) exclaiming, "I've thrown out better things!" I was happy to be back in the Bronx with my friends, and Mama seemed to have gotten back into the swing of life without Papa.

Tess was not working at the Post Office because as soon as World War II ended the women were forced to leave their jobs so men returning from war could go back to work. She still lived at home. She met a fellow named Lester Epstein who lived on East 172nd Street. Within a year, Lester had moved into our house on Manor Avenue, and they took over Mama's bedroom. Mama and I shared a bed in a little room over the stairs that used to be my father's bedroom.

The war was over and as veterans came back home, there wasn't enough affordable housing. The Bronx River Projects were under construction, and Quonset huts filled the area near Soundview Avenue and Clason Point. I was always curious to see the inside of a Quonset hut. My friend Alice and her mother lived in one. I never actually got to go in because her mother was a prostitute and was "busy" every time I went over.

Rent control was in place at that time, and tenants had to move for us to raise the rent. We had a four-family house. All houses with more than two units were subject to rent control. Mama Dora was shrewd, and she knew how to work the system by moving Tess and Lester to a different unit and moving us to another, forcing the tenants that were not family to move. This made the other units decontrolled and we could raise the rent. We moved to a small three-room apartment downstairs in the back. Three rooms were cramped for Mama, Tess, Lester and me. Mama got rid of all the dining room furniture except for the locked china cabinet filled with important papers and family treasures. We slept on a bed together in the living room while Tess and Lester had the only bedroom.

I hated Lester! Mama was not happy having him there, but there was not much she could do about it. She called him, "A real piece of work."

Lester's mother would come over and tell Mama, "Throw the bum out!" While he was sponging off Mama, somehow he always seemed to have enough money for a new car or boat.

Lester liked young girls, and I thought his behavior was disgusting. At one point, he locked himself in the bedroom with two of my friends. Even though he wasn't yet married to Tess, I sensed something was not right and that this was a betrayal to Tess. I confronted him, and he was so angry he slapped me across the face.

My Uncle Abe was the only one I could tell, and he did nothing! Uncle Milton and Aunt Mae were still in the Catskills better known to Jews as the Borscht Belt. He was the only decent man I knew and would have trusted to take care of the problem. This situation with Lester solidified my opinion of men. I knew I had no one to protect me or even to lean on and trust. I was on my own to navigate a world full of snakes.

Roslynne, in high school at James Monroe in 1947.

High School

For years, I had watched Tess and other high school students on the outdoor track of James Monroe High School, which was right across the street from our house. Because we were on the second floor, I was able to sit in the window and dream about the day I would be a high school student. I graduated from PS 77 in January of 1947.

Summer passed and during the next four years as a student at James Monroe High School I left my childhood behind. High school changed my life. On the first day of school, while I was standing at my locker in the basement, a boy came up to me and planted a kiss on my cheek. I was shocked, but I liked the attention. Boys! High school just got a lot more interesting. I was still self-conscious about my broken front tooth, but I had learned to accept what I could not change and celebrate life on my own terms.

We had always been poor, but since Papa's death, money was even tighter. I babysat as often as I could around the neighborhood for twenty-five cents an hour, but I also had to pay for everything I owned. I never managed to have much money for clothes. In fact, I only had two or three pairs of panties that I washed every night and hung over the tub to dry, often running out the door with damp fabric clinging to my bottom. I wore hand-me-downs from Tess or my cousin from Brooklyn. If my shoes had holes in the soles, paying to have them repaired at the shoemaker was not an option. I filled them with cardboard.

I didn't join any extra activities or sports in high school. I did just the bare minimum to get by, anxious to rush home to meet my friends and spend as much time as possible socializing and having fun. Of course, no one at home ever took an interest in my education or encouraged me to study. Since kindergarten, my education was left up to the school and whatever I was able to glean on my own. As a teenager, socializing and belonging to a group, which the Bronx was full of, was my main ambition.

My first real crush, David Weinsoff, was part of the group I hung with. He went to the Bronx High School of Science and was really bright. I was fifteen and he was seventeen. He was smitten by my kisses. What a thrill when he invited me to his prom. I had no gown, shoes or a wrap and had no idea where I would get the money for such luxuries. Mama took me to S. Klein's in Manhattan and we found a gown for five dollars, my entire savings from babysitting. It was way too big, but Mama altered it to fit.

I was riding the trolley wondering how I could possibly afford shoes or a wrap. As if my heart's desires were heard in heaven, I glanced down and there, just below my feet on the trolley floor, was a dollar bill. I picked it up and to my total disbelief, a ten dollar bill was wrapped inside that single! It may have well been a million dollars! I bought a gray wrap and white sandals and felt like I was on top of the world. David left for the summer shortly after prom, and by the time he returned, I was interested in other boys. Boys were definitely interested in me.

The cliques of the Bronx became my life. We did everything together, traveling in groups to movies, dances, soda shops, the beach, or just hanging out. I had blossomed into a sixteen-year-old with a huge personality. I was finally able to get my front tooth capped. I had lived with half of a front tooth and an awkward, self-conscious grin for years, but when I came out of the dentist I felt as though I had emerged into a beautiful princess. I could not stop smiling! I had turned from an ugly duckling into a swan and I felt beautiful. My figure had begun to develop curves that, combined with a vivacious personality I had developed to compensate for my crooked smile, set me free. I was getting a lot of attention from boys and for the first time in my life, I felt happy.

Neighborhood gangs, greasers, and social clubs dominated the Bronx and all of the boroughs when I was in high school. Social clubs were held in the basements of different homes and were rented out as spaces for boys to hang out, smoke, dance and have parties. The boys all wore suits and ties and the girls wore dresses and had their hair in curls, a thin disguise for the raging hormones beneath our finery. Every weekend there was a club looking to fill its walls with girls. There were no such things as chaperones, and smooching and petting was part of the fun. Slow dancing and the Lindy-hop were popular. Our group frequented Club Reverie, and once again, life took a turn.

Nat and me in our teen-aged dating years

Nat Sol Steinberg

One night some fellows from Club Reverie gave me and a friend a lift home, and Nat was in the back seat. The car was packed so I sat in his lap. All the girls thought he was good looking and charming. I thought he was kind of a smart-ass and didn't give him a second glance. He was trying to be witty and I was right there scrapping with him. I don't think Nat was used to girls that talked back. Fate threw us together one night at the club when he was not with his girl, and he asked me to dance. I was sixteen; he was eighteen, six-foot-two with olive skin and very good looking. He was tall, dark and handsome.

He had dropped out of Samuel Gompers Industrial High School for Boys at sixteen. This could have been a red flag because this was a school for special education students, or troubled boys who did not succeed in a typical school setting, and a place where they could learn meaningful trades. He was studying an automotive trade, but it wasn't for him. Nat was charming, a great dancer and very popular. He seemed normal or above average in every way.

Nat's family lived on Allerton Avenue in the Pelham Parkway area, which was a much better neighborhood than mine. His father, Harry, was a Romanian Jew. He was loud, funny and stubborn. Nat's mother, Yetta, was a first generation American; her parents were Russian immigrants. Yetta was born in the United States but raised in Russia. She returned to the United States when she was seventeen. She was a fabulous cook, and I spent a lot of time at their house. They adored Nat, and Yetta referred to him as "My Nat," reminding me of how Mama Dora spoiled my father and had always called him, "My Jankel."

They owned a small kosher chicken shop. Everybody ate chicken for Shabbat, so Nat worked two days a week in the shop selling and flicking chickens. His younger brother, Bernie, was weirdly quiet and his little sister, Shelia, was adorable. Nat and I became inseparable. We were head over heels in love. Mama and Tess never thought he was good enough for me. On the other hand, his parent's also thought I was not good enough for Nat.

When our relationship became serious, Nat told me he had a "big secret." I couldn't imagine what it was. He finally shared the fact that he could not read or write. He had dyslexia. No wonder he was so charismatic and witty. His charm provided a cover so no one would guess his disability. Dyslexia had been diagnosed by that time, but there was not a comprehensive plan to work with people who suffered from this dysfunction. In those days, any abnormalities were hidden in the closet and never discussed, causing needless shame and embarrassment for so many. Nat had bluffed his way through eighteen years of life with charm and bluster. I told him not to worry; I would teach him to read.

Our first attempt at sex was a disaster! Things were not working out for Nat, and he blamed it on me. He said I had a "cross bone" that kept him from being able to penetrate. I was terrified! I knew I was some kind of freak. I had no idea what a cross bone was, much less who I could ask. I suspect lots of my girlfriends were having sex, but we didn't ever discuss it. So many things had gone wrong in my life that I was in a total panic. I had finally found the man for me, but I was disfigured by some weird kind of bone. I was more determined than ever to have sex and prove I was normal!

Nat and I dated steadily for a year. I buckled down to my studies, and I was able to take a co-op course that allowed me to go to school, alternating a week of school with a week of work. We learned how to dress for business, look sophisticated and smart, and how to conduct ourselves in an interview.

At sixteen, I got a job at a fiction book club posting members' accounts. I took the train to Times Square and from there to Canal Street on the tip of Manhattan. I was making twenty-six dollars a week, an enormous sum at that time, certainly the most money I had ever made. My friends and I ate at Horn and Hardart, an automated restaurant that was the most popular place in Manhattan. It was a real treat to eat out. For a nickel or two I could buy a tray of mac and cheese and baked beans; I can still taste how delicious it was.

Life was good. Nat and I were in love, and we had a great group of friends. We were always very social. Nat loved to play cards and was always ready to gamble on what he thought would be a winning hand, but he knew the game of pool was where he could make money. If I needed him, I always knew I could find him at one of the pool halls he frequented. His parents supported him, but Nat loved the art of the hustle.

I graduated from James Monroe High School on my eighteenth birthday, January 2nd, 1951. I was good at math ,and after I had graduated from James Monroe, I went to business school to study typing, stenography, and bookkeeping. Mama Dora was so proud of me and I was happy to make her proud. Mama Dora became a United States citizen, a requirement at that time. Yiddish was still her primary language , and she spoke very broken English. She took the night course offered at James Monroe High School for immigrants and I helped her study. I admired her so much, and I realized how intelligent and capable she was.

That summer Nat went to work as the head waiter in the Webertuck Kosher Hotel in the White Mountains of New Hampshire. His younger brother, Bernie, went along and worked as a bus boy. We missed each other so much that Nat had decided to quit and come back to work at his father's chicken shop in the Bronx. The hotel didn't want to lose him, so they invited me to stay at the hotel for free. I took his little sister, Shelia, and we stayed for the entire summer. I kept busy helping the hotel staff with a variety of jobs.

There were a lot of "old ladies" who summered at the hotel, and much of their day was spent sitting in groups over meals sharing their life stories. I heard, "I could have," "I should have" and "I would have," in every conversation. Those conversations changed me. That summer, I decided that I was never going to live my life with regret. I was not going to be an old woman who sat around and complained about the life I missed. I was going to live!

Back at home, Tess and Lester had a beautiful baby girl, Alexis. Mama Dora was still living in the front apartment so Tess had lots of help with her new baby. I couldn't help but remember what a wonderful mother figure Tess had been to me when she was just fourteen.

Just as the nation was recovering from World War II, we became involved in the Korean War, 1950 to 1953. North Korea invaded South Korea in 1950 and the United States provided eighty-eight percent of the soldiers. Nat was drafted into the Marines. I had kept my promise and helped him learn to read, at least well enough to fill out the basic enlistment forms. He was scheduled to leave at the end of October. I could not imagine life without him and was afraid he would be sent to the front lines in Korea. I had finally found the love of my life and now I was at risk of losing him.

Marriage

We decided to get married before Nat shipped out. We expected him to leave in less than two weeks and we did not expect to have a big wedding. In just a few days, a miracle happened! Yetta, Nat's mother, began planning our wedding the day we told our families we were going to marry. On the other hand, Nat's father, Harry, did everything he could to keep Nat from marrying me. He even offered to buy him a brand new Cadillac!

Yetta, along with many family members and friends, organized a beautiful wedding at Emmanuel Orthodox Synagogue on Elder Avenue and East 172nd Street. Nat's step-grandfather, Rabbi Ruben, officiated and over a hundred and fifty guests attended. We were married on October, twenty-seventh, 1951, just six months after I had graduated from high school.

My graduation photo, 1951

Our family and friends gathered together to make our wedding extraordinary. My childhood friend Marilyn had a bridal shower for me. Aunt Mae's neighbor had a beautiful, size nine wedding gown that fit me perfectly. Family and friends cooked for days to provide a full meal for all of our guests. A friend of Nat's volunteered as our photographer. His friends also served as our groomsmen and doubled as our waiters. My close friend Naomi was my bridesmaid and Aunt Mae was my

Mama Dora at our wedding

matron of honor. Milton and Mae walked me down the aisle.

While it all happened so fast and was wonderfully exciting, I was having second thoughts and Nat was throwing up a week before the wedding. At ages eighteen and twenty-one, I think we were just two scared kids overwhelmed by the unknown future that lay ahead of us.

Yetta insisted on meeting my mother, who I had not seen for years. She was still living at Seabury Place. It was awkward, but thankfully Mother was civil. Grandfather Beresofsky came to the wedding along with my two aunts on my mother's side, Hilda and Lillie. My father and Natalie did not come, which was a disappointment, but not a surprise. All in all, it was a fantastic event, and everyone had a terrific time.

Instead of leaving a few days after the wedding as we had thought, Nat was sent to the Marine Corps Recruit Depot at Parris Island in Port Royal, South Carolina. After training, he was transferred to Marine Corps Base Camp at Camp Lejeune in Jacksonville, North Carolina. He came home on leave, and I told him I was not leaving him again. I was going back to North Carolina with him. I packed my few belongings, said goodbye to Mama Dora and boarded the bus for the South.

Roslynne Jacobs and Nat Sol Steinberg cutting their wedding cake on October twenty-seventh, 1951.

We realized we had no living quarters on the base and were fortunate to meet another Marine and his wife on the bus. They invited us to share their double-wide trailer, which was in a trailer camp set up to house Marines, for a small fee. It was like nothing I had ever experienced, and I had seen a lot! The trailer was filthy. I had grown up in a dirty house so dirt, rats, and cockroaches were not unfamiliar. The oppressive heat, a stinking mattress filled with bedbugs along with portable toilets out back was more than I could bear. Nat was required to live on base but came home on the weekends, and no matter the circumstances we were happy to be together.

Fortunately, I was able to collect unemployment and that allowed me to move into a small trailer of my own. I was a lousy cook. My specialties were French toast and tuna fish but making those dishes in my own small space was wonderful. A tiny store and post office in a trailer park offered the only place to get out of the claustrophobic space. It was not easy for a girl raised in the Bronx to understand the southern drawl. Life moved at a different pace and it was a challenging to be away from the bustle of the city, the Jewish culture and my friends. It was worth it to be near Nat.

Nat was transferred to the Marine Corps Air Station Cherry Point in Havelock, North Carolina. We began to meet a few people from New York and New Jersey and felt like we were more at home. Our new friends invited us to live in a development for Marines, and for the first time since leaving New York, we had friends and community. This was our first real home. I bought some second-hand furniture and we settled into life with evenings of friends, laughter, and canasta.

Nat became a butcher in the commissary. Unfortunately, he still loved to gamble and lost more money than he won. It was a big blow when he lost a hundred and fifty dollars at craps. Nat also had that friendly, bigger than life personality which attracted me to him, but it wasn't a great match for military life. He had just made corporal and the raise in pay was much needed. A lieutenant felt like he was too friendly and had overstepped his rank, and he was demoted to private.

Mark Allen Steinberg

I was expecting! We were thrilled, although I didn't know the first thing about having a baby. Luckily, I was surrounded by other Marine wives who offered me a great deal of mental and emotional support. Our first son, Mark Allen Steinberg, arrived on April 5, 1953. It was Easter Sunday. There was so much fuss over Mark being the first child born on Easter. An announcement in the base paper the *Cherry Point News* read, "The Easter Bunny has arrived" referring to Mark as the bunny's gift. We named him Mark in remembrance of Moisha (Morris,) his grandfather on Nat's side and Allen, for my Grandpa, Elya (Alex).

The *mitzvah of Pidyon Ha'Ben* is a Jewish ceremony, known as the "redemption of the first born son." It is an ancient tradition rooted in the Torah and is a ritual that involves, "Buying the son back from a Kohen," for biblical reasons. Another reason is to remind us of the Exodus from Egypt when God killed the Egyptian firstborn but spared the Jewish firstborn. Also, it is a time to acknowledge that everything we own belongs to God.

This was a very special event in our family, and most of our relatives came to North Carolina for the *Pidyon Ha'Ben*. The only Rabbi that could do the ceremony was fifty miles away, and we were thrilled he could come. Nat's parents, Harry, and Yetta, along with his aunt and siblings, Bernie and Shelia, arrived. Many of his cousins came. Mama Dora arrived with Uncle Milton and Mae and my cousins, Clifford and Howard.

I hadn't seen Mama Dora for a year-and-a-half. She was very thin, pale and more tired than I had ever seen her. She was greatly relieved to see that I was not mentally ill. She was so afraid that I would suffer from the same mental issues my mother had developed after I was born. My father came from

Chattanooga, Tennessee. By this time, we had many Jewish friends and neighbors who also came to celebrate our firstborn son.

While Nat and I were enjoying being parents and finding our place in our new community, life, as we knew it in the Bronx, was changing. Mae had fallen in love with an Italian man, which utterly shattered Milton. This was so shocking and made me so sad because they had always been an example of a stable marriage. I hurt for Uncle Milton, who was the anchor in our family.

Soon after Mama Dora returned to the Bronx from the *Pidyon Ha'Ben*, she got very sick and went to see Doctor Adair, a cancer specialist. The diagnosis was stomach cancer. The family wanted me to come back to Manor Avenue and care for her, but I was not ready to leave Nat and Mark, who was barely two months old. Lester and Tess were still living in the back apartment at Manor Avenue. Uncle Abe, Tess, and Uncle Milton, who still lived just around the block, came often to help take care of Mama Dora.

In October of 1953, Mama Dora died. I came home for her funeral, and she was buried at Mount Moriah with Elya. An era had ended. My beloved grandparents, the only parents I had ever known, were gone.

Back to our Roots

The Korean War ended and Nat was discharged in 1954. Nat's father Harry, Uncle Milton and Lester drove down to North Carolina to load our belongings on a trailer for our move back to 1320 Manor Avenue. Our prize possession was a new wringer washer from Montgomery Wards that we brought back with us to replace the heavy porcelain sink mounted to the wall of the kitchen. We settled into Mama Dora's apartment, back to the cockroaches, mice, and ancient furniture. It was nice to have Tess as a next door neighbor and be home with family back in the Bronx.

Nat had a lot of experience as a butcher in the Marine commissary, but it was tough to get a job if you weren't in a union. Uncle Abe said we didn't have to pay rent until we got on our feet. Nat's father was glad to have him back at the chicken shop, and I stayed home to raise Mark.

Nat still loved to gamble and poker was a weekly event. Our house was always filled with characters that Nat invited over for gambling. My job was to make brisket and serve sandwiches on rye with kosher pickles. Nat always brought home free meat, and I cooked a big brisket to serve to the crowd. I made twenty-five dollars for the evening because all the guys chipped in for a meal, which really helped us make ends meet. Free meat, feeding the poker players and food from our in-laws got us through.

Nat was not making any headway getting into the union. Yetta took the bull by the horns and paid a personal visit to Benny Levine, head of the kosher butcher's union. I have no idea what she said, but shortly after her visit, Nat was given an apprenticeship in the butcher's union. He learned the trade of a kosher butcher and earned his place in the Union along with a pay raise. We decided it was time for Mark to have a sibling.

We had talked about having enough kids to make our own baseball team.

Grandma Dora's estate was not settled until about a year after we came back from North Carolina. Just before she died she named Uncle Abe as the executor of her estate. Abe was a good choice as executor because he had always put family first. He had Lillie transferred to a hospital in the Bronx. He looked after Lillie after Papa died and when Mama was no longer able to do so. When Mama's estate was finally settled, a small amount of money was divided among Abe, my father, Lillie (for her continuing care), Mae and Tess. It was up to Mama Dora's children to share with their children as they chose. Dear old dad never shared a dime with me. Uncle Abe and Mae chipped in and gave me a share of their money.

Two More Wonderful Sons

Donald Robert Steinberg arrived February 7, 1956. Donald was named after Mama Dora. We were so happy to have a brother for Mark, and I was always partial to boys. We had the *briss* (circumcision for Jewish male babies) at the house where many of our relatives and friends met Donald for the first time. As time would tell, Mark loved Donald and took the role of big brother seriously. Nat and I were happy to have a growing family, and we all loved Donald's outgoing and intelligent character.

Six months after Donald was born I became pregnant again! We were surprised but happy. Stephen Howard Steinberg was born on June 4, 1957, and three boys kept me busy full time. Stephen was born with bowed legs, and he wore braces all day and all night only taking them off to bathe until he was about four years old. At night, he wore tiny shoes connected by a bar to keep his legs straight. It was always

Our three boys: Mark Allen 9, Donald Robert 6, and Stephen Howard 4$^{1/2}$.

astonishing to watch how fast he could get around with those braces.

Stephen was a good boy and he adored his brothers. For reasons, we still don't understand, Stephen didn't speak until he was four years old. I took him to a specialist who assured me not to worry; it was just a long phase of baby talk. Because Stephen and Donald were only fourteen months apart, I had a twin carriage for them and we walked everywhere. We often walked to the Bronx Zoo, which was four miles away, and I always wore high heels.

Nat was in the butcher's union and worked more than full time. A generation later the neighborhood had gone through many changes. After World War II, there was a great exodus of the Jewish population from the Bronx, replaced with Puerto Ricans, African Americans, and West Indians. Westchester Avenue lost many of the small mom and pop shops, the stores of my youth. The days of kids filling the streets for games of curb ball and hopscotch had ended as the streets became filled with cars.

Mark went to PS 77 and even had the same teacher that I did. Nat was as social as ever and we always had a full house on the weekends. Milton and Mae had gotten back together and moved to Flushing, Queens, to a brand new apartment house. They came over often with Clifford and Howard, now teenagers. Abe and Jean moved in upstairs with their son, Norman, and daughter Carol. Tess and Lester decided to move to Florida to manage a boarding house Lester's mother owned.

Life was changing and we were growing up. But some things never changed. Out of the blue, I got a call from the police department saying, "Come and get her." My mother, who I had not seen for years, had left the water on in her apartment in Seabury place. It had not only flooded her apartment but was now flooding the downstairs. There was no answer when the neighbors called or knocked. The building super called the

Roslynne with Donald, Stephen and Mark on the steps of Mark's school, PS77 in the Bronx, where she had gone to school also.

police who knocked on the door with no reply. They had no choice but to kick in the door. As they crashed through, they were met by my mother who was standing on the other side of the door with a pot of boiling water that she heaved in the face of the officers.

She was taken to the mental ward of a local hospital. I have no idea why she put my name on the list as a person to call. When I saw her, she acted as though nothing had happened. I called her brother, Harry, who came to sign her out of the mental ward. I visited her for Mother's Day with the children, and she began talking about her, "little girl," not realizing I was standing in front of her. I continued to visit Mother with all three children as often as I could, saddened to see her deteriorating state of mind.

Donald, sitting next to his mother, on his last trip to the Bronx Zoo with his brothers, Stephen on the left, and Mark. Donald was diagnosed with childhood leukemia and was only six years and four months old when he died in 1962.

Heartbreak

We were a happy family. Our three rambunctious boys kept me busy. When Donald was about six years old, I noticed he was more tired than usual. The boys with their wrestling and rough and tumble play were always bruised, but Donald was getting bruised in a way that went beyond typical. The smallest bruise would turn to a deep purple-black. I took him to the doctor who sent me on to Grand Central Hospital. There was no conversation or discussion about why we needed a specialist at the hospital; we just followed the doctor's orders.

We took the train to Grand Central Hospital in Manhattan. In those days, parents waited downstairs in the lobby while patients were seen. I waited for hours becoming more concerned as every hour passed while Donald was upstairs with a specialist. Finally, the lobby phone rang, and when I answered the doctor said, "Mrs. Steinberg, your son is in deep trouble."

I will never forget those words. My stomach dropped to my feet as I asked, "What is wrong with him? Can we fix it?"

All he said was, "He has acute leukemia and maybe ten days to live."

I was stunned, shocked and in a state of disbelief. My world was reeling. I could not believe what I was hearing. I was alone. My precious child was upstairs, and I heard a voice over the phone telling me my child, my Donald, was going to die?! I went completely numb, heartache lodged in the pit of my soul.

I remember walking out of the hospital sobbing and gasping for a breath. I found myself in Times Square, confused and dazed. I could not stop crying and shaking. I don't ever remember feeling that helpless in my entire life. The chutzpah, resolve and resilience that I had been able to call on in the most difficult times of my life were gone. My heart was broken.

Somehow, I found myself back at the hospital. I don't even remember calling anyone, but thankfully Abe arrived, and we went upstairs to see Donald. Donald was cheerful, and I thought I had misunderstood everything. My Donald could not possibly die. A hematologist came in and my hope soared; I prayed for a miracle. There were more questions than answers, and as we left Donald's hospital room, Abe broke down in the hallway.

Dealing With Tragedy

Life from that day forward changed for all of us. Leukemia is a cancer that starts in blood-forming tissue, such as the bone marrow and causes large numbers of abnormal blood cells to be produced and enter the bloodstream. At that time, there were not the advanced treatment options we have available today. Donald stayed at Grand Central Hospital for weeks. I spent every night at the hospital with him. Nat and I were grateful for the support of family and friends. Donald started bleeding from the nose and losing a lot of blood. He needed continual transfusions.

Shortly before Donald became sick, Nat teamed up with a childhood friend and they opened R&E Kosher Meats. Nat stayed busy running the new business, and all of his time and energy went into making the business succeed. He became distant and emotionally unavailable at a time when I was at home with three boys and we all needed him more than ever. The summer before, I had gotten into a terrible fight with my in-laws, and my relationship with them was shattered.

When the grand opening of the store was held, we fell into each other's arms as we realized the value of family. I was so grateful to have my in-laws close as we all suffered in our own way through this challenging time with Donald.

Nat's butcher's union and many friends and relatives as well as the local firemen donated blood. Yetta and Harry stayed at our house to help with Mark and Stephen. Uncle Milton bought Donald a little portable television so he could watch his favorite show, *The Merry Mailman*, starring Ray Heatherton. It was a children's show that entertained audiences with games, songs, stories, puppets and magic tricks. At that time, Ray Heatherton was one of the most beloved TV personalities. It was a bright spot in Donald's life.

One day, Donald had been sleeping and he woke up to find that he had slept through an episode of *The Merry Mailman*. He was so upset it took four nurses to calm him down, necessary because we were afraid he would begin hemorrhaging. The TV station was located across the street from the hospital, and I was determined to make Donald as happy as possible. I called the studio to tell them about our story, and to my delight and surprise Ray Heatherton came to the hospital the next day to see Donald. He was delighted! Ray left a huge bag of toys for Donald, including "Robbie the Robot." Donald was so happy! Media coverage of the event brought a lot of attention to the issue of children's leukemia and many new followers to *The Merry Mailman*.

I had not been home in weeks to see my dear boys, and Donald missed his brothers. Uncle Milton brought Mark and Stephen up for a visit. Donald was so good-natured, as he took the toys he had been given, and one-at-a-time gave them to his brothers, happy to share. One of my dearest treasures is a happy, pencil drawing Donald made of a clown and other things he saw from his hospital bed. He called it "The Flying Attractions." It is a bitter-sweet memory that takes me back to that hospital bed like it was yesterday. Eventually, Donald was in remission, and we were able to go home for a short while. The Leukemia Society sent a social worker to help with the family. We tried to make his life as normal as possible and to celebrate every moment.

Nat was working very long hours but came home at night and on the weekends. I was trying to deal with Donald's loss and still be a good mother and wife. Nat was not able to cope emotionally with the situation and was unable to express his needs. He often had difficulty expressing any emotion, sorrow or joy. I was dying emotionally and needed his support, and I began to resent the distance between us.

After a short stay at home, Donald had to return to the hospital where he lapsed into a coma. Somehow I felt complicit in his suffering. As his mother, I thought that I was supposed to be able to stop it. My mind, knowing this was out of my control, and my heart, aching at my inability to protect him, were miles apart.

He had struggled many times before, and I always begged, "Come back; come back. Mommy is here." This time, I knew it was time to let him go. I comforted myself by knowing he wasn't in Europe and he wouldn't be murdered, tortured or experimented on at the hands of the Nazis. I was helpless to end his suffering and make him well. It wasn't supposed to be like this. My grief was unbearable.

Nat and I were at Donald's side when he died on Saturday, June 30, 1962. He had lived almost five months longer than the doctor predicted, and we were grateful for every moment. Our dear Donald was buried the next day, in a small white casket at Mount Moriah with Papa Alex and Mama Dora.

A creative drawing Donald made of a clown and other things he saw from his bed at Grand Central Hospital. He called it "The Flying Attractions."

Never Forgotten

Life never returned to normal, but the days passed. July arrived and Yetta arranged for Mark and Stephen to go to summer camp. I desperately needed something to keep me occupied, so I went to work in the butcher shop while Nat buried himself in his work. I wasn't really suited for butcher shop work, but I was glad to be busy. I saw an ad for a furrier in Manhattan needing a bookkeeper, so I applied. I was hired as a bookkeeper and also modeled furs for the customers.

Nat never talked about Donald, his feelings, my feelings, or how losing Donald had affected our marriage, and our family. I was feeling lonely and disconnected in my marriage and when I needed emotional support from my husband, he was not able to give it. I became more lonesome as the days and weeks passed while Nat spent his free time watching television. Donald's passing affected all of us. Once again, I lost touch with Mother because I just did not have the emotional energy to deal with my loss and her emotional needs.

Mark was nine years old. He was not a good student, was very hard-headed and often got into fights. Fist fights were not uncommon in those days and were often used to settle arguments. One day he came home and asked, "Mommy, did Uncle Bernie kill Jesus?" A classmate had told Mark his Uncle Bernie had killed Jesus. Mark let his fists speak for him, insisting that his Uncle Bernie did not kill Jesus. Mark asked me who Jesus was, certain his Uncle had never killed anyone. I told him, as Jews, we believed Jesus was a prophet, but not the son of God as Christians believed.

I understood Mark's difficulty in losing his brother; I was still dealing with my own loss and had a hard time coping with Mark's behavior. Stephen was always patient and quiet. He was always good and never complained about anything.

There was such a contrast in their personalities, but I loved both boys equally.

That summer, my father and Natalie agreed to keep Mark for a few weeks at their home in Chattanooga, Tennessee. Natalie did the best thing she had ever done for our family when she helped Mark with his math. When he returned, we enrolled him in the Cub Scouts, and I became a den mother.

Nat left early for work and returned late. I felt like my life was an upheaval of circumstance ruled by chance as I tried to cope with Donald's loss. I desperately needed the emotional support of my husband, but Nat had nothing to give. He withdrew, and although we had never talked about our emotions, communication on all levels evaporated.

Unfinished portrait of Donald between his adult brothers

Rochdale Village

In 1964, the burden of so many memories of losing people I loved at 1320 Manor Avenue became unbearable. I had to move. I signed up for a co-op apartment, which was offered on a sliding scale, at a new development called Rochdale Village in Jamaica, Queens. It was a huge new high-rise complex that offered a "lifestyle" and was not just a place to live. Rochdale Village was a city within a city. The residents were mostly Jewish. There was a school on the premises and the first enclosed mall in New York City.

A massive new red brick high-rise development, soon to be our new home, arose out of the earth at angles on the site of the former Jamaica Race Track. It was so big that it had six-thousand apartment units. Aside from just the physical changes of living in a high-rise at Rochdale Village, this was a period of time when I experienced enormous personal growth. I grew in self-confidence and became and independent woman.

We had never had a brand new apartment. It was large, open and absolutely spotless – such a change from Manor Avenue! Our second-floor apartment opened into a large living room, a big dining room, and a huge kitchen. We even had a terrace, a perfect place to enjoy breakfast and entertain guests. I loved living in a brand new apartment!

It was an enjoyable distraction from recent sorrows, and I felt like our brand new home, new furniture, and new surroundings offered us a chance to breathe new life and hope to our family. This was our opportunity for a new beginning. We found out that Nat's cousins, Joanie, and Morty, lived in the same building. We became fast friends, and the four of us spent many evenings playing pinochle.

I really wanted a color T.V., a brand new concept at that time. I even had dreams our black and white T.V. turned into color, but I had to choose between drapes or a new T.V. I wanted a beautiful home, something I had never had, so I chose new drapes. They were custom designed "window treatments" and cost a whopping five hundred dollars, an enormous sum of money at that time.

A few months had passed and the mall merchants had a contest to win a color T.V. I entered daily with no doubt that I would win. I still had the uncanny knack for sensing when something was going to happen. Good or bad, I could always feel when a change was in the air. I was on the phone with Nat one day when I told him that I needed to hang up. I'd had a premonition that I had won the contest, and we were going to have a new T.V. With his usual disgust for my opinions, he said I was crazy.

Moments later there was a heavy knock at the door. I opened it in anticipation and the man said, "Are you, Rose Steinberg?" I nodded and he said, "Congratulations, you have won a brand new color television!" It was the largest T.V. made at that time. It brought me back to the moment I found the dollar with a ten dollar bill inside on the trolley floor.

As fabulous as life was at Rochdale Village when we settled into our new home, something was still missing. We had more material things than either of us had ever dreamed of, but even with our new home, Nat and I grew farther apart. Nat continued to spend from dawn to dusk at work, and when he was home, he sat in front of the television like a robot, shutting out his family. His foul language, derogatory remarks, and constant put-downs, directed at me, became a routine. I felt like I was trapped in an invisible cage. The weight of his constant judgment and disrespect left me feeling more isolated than ever.

It became evident that we all needed more therapy. Stephen had a very hard time adjusting to school and everyday life. He was my child with a quiet and easy going personality, such a sweet soul. When I would ask how he was, he would say, "I need help."

Mark had an outgoing personality and he loved his collection of lizards and snakes. My father and Natalie had come for a visit, and Mark was so mad he had to give up his room for them that he let one of his snakes loose in the living room. I was concerned this might be more than typical boy mischief and that Mark might be acting out to cover his pain at losing his brother. Maybe I could not see through my own veil of hurt. Whatever the reason, we all needed professional help to deal with issues from losing Donald.

It was not in Nat's makeup to discuss issues or how he felt about Donald's death. I felt like when we talked, I never could reach his soul. As for me, there was no doubt I was still wrestling with Donald's loss. I had become neurotic and fearful that if the children were sick or injured they might have leukemia, and I was taking them to the doctor far too often.

Rochdale Village had many services and one of those was family counseling offered through the school system. Nat didn't go for long and never had much to say about the experience. Mark was a teenager and I felt like therapy helped, but it was hard to tell. Stephen grew and learned from the experience. After therapy, he asked for guitar lessons and was moving forward, growing and learning. There was nothing that could heal the ache in my heart from losing Donald. As I write this, after eighty-two years, I still feel the pain of his loss.

I was in my mid-thirties and had still never learned to drive. I was feeling boxed in at home, so I was very excited to be invited for a shopping trip to A & S Department Store with two women I had met at the village. I was a "rough around the edges" girl from the Bronx, and I thought they were very sophisticated. The air was thick with something odd between them from the moment I got in the car. That feeling that something wasn't right was lodged in the pit of my stomach, but I was shamelessly intoxicated at the thought of being accepted by stylish, wealthy women so I ignored my feelings.

On the way home from our shopping trip, they began to laugh and celebrate their success, and I realized I had been roped into a shoplifting trip. They had stolen clothes and jewelry from the store. I was shocked and embarrassed, and at the same time so grateful they hadn't been caught. Needless to say, I never went out with them again, and I was back in my cage, trying to find an identity that was beyond the girl struggling to survive the streets of the Bronx.

Nat was becoming increasingly rude at the card games we hosted, especially around the other men. He wanted his buddies to believe I was a pretty, stay at home wife who was completely subservient and waited on him hand and foot. Nat went from withdrawn to abusive. He would yell, "Hey, cunt, get the food out here, now!" I thought this was my role in life, especially when the other wives said their husbands wished they were more like me. My heart was breaking. I was surrounded by new belongings, but I was lonelier than ever, desperate to find my own identity.

One day Nat came home and said, "I am no longer a partner in the butcher shop. I sold my share of the business to Joe for fifteen-hundred dollars." I was furious! How dare he make this kind of decision without as much as a word to me? To Nat, my life was nothing more than being a subservient housewife.

Nat wasn't mean, he never hit me; he supported our family financially; he just ignored me. It didn't matter if I ranted or raved or was completely quiet. He shut me out. He was a lump in front of the T.V. or he left the house. There was zero communication between us, and I had no idea how to change our situation. I felt like I was dying a slow death but could not put my finger on a specific reason. I didn't know what was missing or how to fix it. I just knew I felt lonely and that life had more to offer.

Because Nat was in the kosher butcher's union, it wasn't long before he found another job. Mark and Stephen had grown from young boys to teenagers, and they were more interested in their friends. School and play occupied most of their time. I found myself longing for intellectual stimulation and the desire to use my life for something greater than being a housewife.

Life at Rochdale had its challenges. To say it was huge is an understatement. It was a vast and imposing complex of apartments and buildings as far as the eye could see. There were extensive hallways that seemed to stretch for miles and come together in massive lobbies. As with all neighborhoods, there are always some people up to no good.

One afternoon I was returning from the laundry, which was on the main level of our wing, when three huge black boys in their late teens approached. The hair stood up on the back of my neck; an ominous feeling overcame me. They looked my way and whispered to each other. I was headed toward the elevator with my basket of laundry and realized I would be trapped. I immediately started to move toward the front of the building where I might be more visible, trying not to draw attention. I could sense their approach and suddenly I was surrounded. One of them, at least six feet, snickered as I felt a huge hand grab my ass. You never know what you'll do until you find yourself in this kind of mess!

I spun around and yelled, "What the hell do you think you are doing?" I felt myself flush with rage as I yelled, "Get the fuck out of here!!!" The feisty kid from the Bronx was back. I was so hostile that it had an immediate effect on their bravado. The most aggressive one flinched and recoiled when I turned and yelled right at him with more aggression than he had. His friends took note and quickly turned and left. The seed of change was planted in my heart. I knew it was time to leave Rochdale Village.

Mark was almost thirteen and his Bar Mitzvah was approaching. He was training with Rabbi Martin David Kahane, also known as Meir Kahane. Little did we know that Meir Kahane would become a Jewish militant and an extreme, right-wing, political activist. He was eventually killed by an Arab gunman.

Mark's Bar Mitzvah was an expensive occasion, three-thousand dollars at that time. I decided to take a job at McCrory's Five-and-Dime Store to save for the event. I wasn't happy, feeling I had more potential than being a sales person behind the counter, so I quit after about four months. Fate intervened and my life changed when I saw a sign in the mall advertising, "Mall Secretary Wanted."

Mark's Bar Mitzva: Harry and Yetta Steinberg; Nat, Roslynne, Mark, and Stephen Steinberg;, Natalie and Jack Jamieson, April 1966

Housewife to Career Woman

I interviewed with Mr. Crackavaner and was hired. I was thrilled! Finally, I had a purpose. I had an outlet for my talents and secretarial skills. I loved being around people and having a mission. This was a long needed turning point in my life. Mr. Crackavaner had come from Roosevelt Field Shopping Mall in Westbury, Long Island. It was the largest shopping mall in New York, one of the largest in the country, and managed by Feist and Feist.

I wasn't just a secretary. I was a secretary in an exciting, fast-paced, growing industry with a boss that I could learn from. He called for a meeting of the local merchants association at a nearby hotel, and I served as secretary for the event. My short-hand and business training came in handy. I was rusty but willing to learn on the job, and soon I was chosen to be the secretary of the merchant's association. I was in heaven! I think I had ignored (or maybe I didn't understand) the need to be something other than a housewife. My whole life had a renewed sense of purpose now that I was working full time. I loved dressing up, wearing heels and looking good. Nat didn't care what I did or didn't do; communication between us ceased to exist.

I began developing an assertive part of myself after a lifetime of being subservient. For the first time in my life, other than being a wife and mother, I felt like I had value and purpose. Just three or four months after first serving as secretary, Mr. Crackavaner died of a heart attack. The work still needed to be done, and I stepped up to the plate. When calls came in for maintenance, I assigned the staff. I managed the books and took over Mr. Crackavaner's role in the office until management could bring in new staff.

The United Housing Foundation hired Feist and Feist as its management team. They sent in Mr. Nass to set up the books and he taught me a lot. They hired a promotional consultant named Selma Friedman. My life changed when she saw my potential and became my mentor.

Selma Friedman was an exceptional woman and the epitome of an educated, savvy female entrepreneur. She was well dressed, attractive, poised and confident, qualities I admired. What made her extraordinary was the fact that she wore braces required by multiple sclerosis, and she never complained or talked about her illness.

It was the mid-sixties. Women in America were expected to devote their lives to being homemakers and caring for their husbands and children. This was the only model I had seen growing up. Until Selma Friedman walked into my life, I thought the problem was with me. I thought that I was abnormal for wanting to use my skills and education for something bigger. I thought maybe I was crazy for enjoying the excitement and feeling a sense of accomplishment and fulfillment that I got from work. I also felt a little guilty because my work was a hell of a lot more satisfying than my marriage.

Granted, I was a secretary, one of the few "acceptable" roles for women at that time. Selma was the founder and owner of Selma Friedman Associates, a shopping center marketing and promotion firm. She was ten years older than I was ,and her confidence was inspiring. I don't know if this opportunity was luck or chance, but my life would never be the same. I knew I had the desire and the training to create a better life for myself. Now I finally had the opportunity.

Betty Friedan was a leading activist for a group of women that would become known as "The Feminist Movement" or "Women's Liberation Movement." Life was changing for women across the nation, and I was thrilled to jump on board. I wasn't a man hater, and I dearly loved my children (women were accused of such things in those days), but I knew that I was more than a wife and homemaker. Fitting in and living up to society's definition of me has never been where I have functioned best. I know I am a dreamer and following those dreams is where I have always felt like my best self. It was never clearer to me than when I began to see the difference I could make at work, and I realized my own potential.

Nat was traveling as a butcher working for Blue Ribbon Kosher Meats in Co-op City. The more I grew into my job and accepted expanded responsibilities, the less I became interested in Nat's job. Mark and Stephen were busy with school. I was never more excited for the chance to jump into work, learn and grow.

Part of my role was showing available spaces in the mall. King George Restaurants was one of the first tenants to sign-up. The next day I received two dozen roses from George, owner of King George's, another affirmation that I was moving in the right direction. My former boss at McCrory's became president of the Rochdale Merchants Association, and I was serving as the secretary and learning about marketing and promotions from Selma. I dove into work and took advantage of every opportunity to learn. I still had the same drive and ambition as that kid up at six in the morning to maximize my opportunity for free ice cream and collect "lucky sticks." This time the stakes were bigger.

One of the first big events we organized at the mall was a contest to paint three Beetle Volkswagens, so popular in the sixties. We did print and radio publicity, and the mall was packed with eager crowds. It was the wind beneath my wings and I knew a career in promotions and events was where I needed to be. I was promoted to assistant to the mall manager and became the marketing director of the mall association. From cosmetic demonstrations to automobile shows and art shows, I promoted events large and small, and the mall attendance grew steadily. I wrote a column, "News from the Rochdale Merchants" for the local paper, and my responsibilities were steadily growing along with crowds in the mall.

One of the women I had met on the "shopping heist" asked me if she could hold an event offering tips on artificial flower arrangements, which were very popular at the time. Reluctantly, I gave her permission.

The last day of the event, she came to me and said, "How the hell did you get this job? I used to eat people like you for breakfast!" I learned that my instincts were good, and from there on if I had a bad feeling about someone, they would not be given the time of day.

OCTOBER, 1968

News From The Rochdale Merchants

By Roslyn Steinberg

LADIES! How would you like to be made up professionally and look more beautiful? Mrs. Lynda Lesce, cosmetician for the Co-op pharmacy, has graciously offered her services to you.

A cosmetic demonstration will be held on October 26th in the enclosed mall at 3 p.m. Mrs. Lesce will demonstrate how you can be a more beautiful you. I urge all you gals to attend this most informative cosmetic show.

COME TO THE 1969 AUTOMOBILE SHOW at the Rochdale Shopping Center. You can see the fabulous 1969 cars in our very own mall. Not only will you see beautiful cars on display, but you will have an opportunity to enter the various contests that each dealer will be holding. The show will run from October 21 thru October 28. See exciting new Dodge, Ford, Buick, Chevrolet and Chrysler cars.

On November 11 there will be an art show in the Shopping Centers. Artists will display their work, and many paintings will be for sale. If you are looking for a painting, take advantage of this opportunity. If you would like to display some paintings please call 276-6165.

Darkness Revisited

I heard through my Uncle Abe that Hilda, my mother's sister, who was supposedly normal, had committed suicide. Once again, that sickening feeling that this too would be my fate arose from the pit of my stomach. The genetic possibility that I might fall victim to mental illness terrified me. Just when I felt like my life was moving forward, I began feeling insecure and afraid.

As Mother's next of kin, Harry, my mother's brother who took care of her, asked me to sign papers which would allow my mother to sell the property in New Berlin, New York. When I refused, he offered me a few thousand dollars. We needed the money, but I felt like I would be selling my soul for a few grand, so I said no. I also feared I would become responsible for Mother, and I knew that would be emotional suicide.

Even though I couldn't afford it, I knew I need counseling. Hilda's suicide rocked me to the core. It had never occurred to me that mental illness could emerge in an older adult. I think I had associated childbirth (mine) as the whole reason my mother became mentally ill. Mama Dora always lived with the fear that I would inherit this mental illness. I got scared after Hilda's suicide that maybe this insanity would come after me. At that time, mental illness was a taboo subject in polite society. It was considered a shameful depravity to be kept behind closed doors.

By this time, I had spent years feeling forlorn and miserable. Being rejected by my father and estranged from my mother had taken its toll on my spirit. I found the rejection along with the fear of becoming mentally ill like my mother or her sisters disabling. Though I felt insecure and unhappy in my marriage, I was a fighter. The scrappy kid from the Bronx was not yet ready to give in. After a lifetime of rejection, I didn't give a damn what anybody thought. I didn't care; I was desperate for help.

I had heard about a psychologist named Dr. Seretsky from a friend. I took the train to Cedarhurst for a year of private counseling followed by six months of group counseling with Dr. Seretsky. Counseling opened a new world for me. I became confident in myself and realized that just because my mother and aunts were mentally ill, it would not necessarily be my destiny.

As angst was tearing at my soul, an unrelenting smoldering darkness ruled my life. I think these sessions with Dr. Seretsky were opening doors and areas of my life I had shut out just to survive. Or maybe I had closed the door to things that were just too hard to remember.

The Dream

Relief came unexpectedly by way of a dream. I recalled a traumatic experience, and it was a memory that was life changing. I woke up at five in the morning, soaked from head to toe in sweat, my heart racing. I had full recall of the terrifying dream, a nightmare, I had just experienced. It was very different from other dreams because I remembered the whole dream in vivid detail.

I was a baby, so present in that moment that I knew I had not imagined this nightmare. I went back in time to a moment in my early childhood and re-lived the moment! I was so hungry, and I could I smell the milk. I felt my lips pucker and then a great love and tenderness from my aunt Tess, who was my caretaker. She had, in many ways, become a mother figure in my life. I felt fabric flutter over my face, and then I was gasping for air. Suddenly my soul was terrified! I was a baby again, utterly overwhelmed with terror as I relived the horror of my mother's insanity.

Aunt Tess told me she was wheeling me in the carriage when Mother came down the street and wanted to hold me. Tess, who was fourteen or fifteen at the time, handed me to her. In the blink of an eye, my sense of love changed to sheer terror. A violent episode had suddenly overtaken Mother. I remembered being held close to her and squeezed, squeezed tighter and tighter. I could not catch my breath. More than the crushing embrace, I remember love changing to terror in the depths of my being as Mother attempted to smother me.

My mother tried to kill me! Aunt Tess wrestled me from her arms and panic filled my soul. I am not sure where that memory went, or where a child can put that kind of hurt. It was years later before it all came rushing back at me with the force of a typhoon.

I had never experienced fear that intense. I called Tess, shaking as I told her about my nightmare. I asked, "Did something awful happen to me when I was a baby?"

She verified everything I had said. In a panic, I called Doctor Seretsky early that morning and asked, "Is it possible to go back to early childhood and recall a memory?"

He said, "Yes."

My anxiety was clear, and I was given an appointment for later that morning. As horrible as it was to remember and re-live the nightmare, it freed me from a dark emotion I must have been holding in my heart. A nervous tic I had developed as a child and that had plagued me for more than thirty years completely disappeared when I remembered the incident.

While it took me years to remember that incident, from the day my mother tried to smother me as a child I remained constantly terrified of her. As I grew older, if I saw her coming I would run and hide. She became stranger by the day. She dressed oddly, wearing very child-like clothes, always with saddle shoes. Her gait went from a normal walk to an odd half-tiptoe with a side-to-side up and down motion. I could see her coming blocks away.

There was no one to tell about my fear, and no one seemed to notice my suffering. Life for everyone was in the throes of the Depression, and I'm sure the adults were just trying to survive. At a very early age, I knew I was on my own. I never held a grudge against Mother because I understood that she was sick, but I also knew enough to avoid her. I became a master of invisibility, hiding in alleys, the shadows of doorways and behind trees or in bushes. I was always feeling paranoid that she was coming to hurt me.

Healing

I had been afraid to learn to drive and decided it was time. I had really never needed to learn and dreaded Nat teaching me and demanding, "Do this; do that," in his demeaning tone that always left me feeling stupid. I finally had the confidence to face my fears and open new doors. I signed up for driving school, and the freedom I found having a car was incredible.

Nat was in a terrible auto accident as he headed to the Bronx in our station wagon. It had been snowing heavily and a truck rear-ended him on the icy roads. He was transported to the hospital black and blue, with an injured back. Thankfully, he was sent home the next day to recover, and I cared for him through a prolonged recovery. Our insurance agent suggested we hire an lawyer, which we did. We hired Attorney Harold Gordon. A year-and-a-half later, we were awarded ten-thousand dollars, enough money for us to buy our first home.

After Mark's Bar Mitzva in 1966, the Steinbergs took a trip through the Smokey Mountains to Chattanooga, Tennessee, and on to Florida to visit family and to sail on a cruiseship.

Nat fully healed from the accident. Mark, thirteen, had a wonderful Bar Mitzvah. His mischievous personality was a magnet for friends. Stephen, our quiet natured son, at just nine years old, was much taller than Mark, making him look like an older brother. He was doing well and had adjusted to life without Donald.

Our station wagon was totaled in the accident, and we got a new Bonneville. We decided to take the boys on a motor trip to Tennessee to explore Gatlinburg, in the Smokey Mountains. I was still on pins and needles around my father and Natalie, but I knew how important it was for the boys to spend time with their grandfather.

Nat and I had grown no closer, but it was what it was. After a brief visit with my father and Natalie, we drove down to Florida to see Tess, Lester and their three children, Alexis, Doreen and Robert. It was wonderful to see them. We headed on to Miami Beach for a four-day cruise on a ship.

A Home of Our Own

In 1968, we left Rochdale Village and moved into our first house with the money we received from the insurance company. I was thirty-five years old. Aside from the short time that I had lived in a tiny trailer, this was the first time in my life I was in a home without next door neighbors separated by a thin wall. It was a Cape Cod style home built in the 1940s in North Valley Stream on 106 Alden Avenue. We put ten thousand down on the purchase price of twenty-seven thousand dollars. I resigned my position at Rochdale Shopping Center and was hopeful life would be better now that we finally had a home of our own.

Our new house was a "handy man special" and neither of us was especially handy. We invested every dime we had to buy the house, and there was nothing left for repairs. Harry and Yetta bought us a refrigerator, and we were always waiting for Nat's "next paycheck" to buy groceries.

Stephen, now twelve years old and in middle school, was next in line for a Bar Mitzvah. He was still our introspective, quiet son who loved to read and was so easy to get along with. He wanted a dog, so we got our first family pet from the animal shelter, an enormous white dog he named Lloyd. Sadly, Lloyd was killed in traffic just a few months after we got him. JC Penny had a pet department at that time. Stephen found a Collie. It was a small, frisky puppy he decided to call Darren. He was so happy and devoted to that dog. Friends gave us a Siamese cat, and eventually we adopted a Doberman. Nat brought him home without asking me first. I hated that dog because he was aggressive and frightened me. Even the previous owners who raised him from a puppy were afraid of him.

Mark had grown into a handsome teenager with a big fun loving personality that girls adored. He was on the wrestling team and had a lot of friends. I was concerned about his academic future. He had no interest in studying and showed no signs of caring how it might affect his future. Social life continued to be the main reason he went to school.

Expenses were mounting, and it was time for me to go back to work. I enjoyed working, but I wanted a job where I could use the skills I had developed at the mall. I took a job at an insurance company doing claims. It was so boring, but I was able to save a little money. A gal from work had a father who was a house painter who gave us a great deal on painting our house, so at least it had some perks. Even though I was driving, one car made life difficult, especially since I only had it on Saturdays.

Nat had taken a second job in Brooklyn with a man named Ludwig, a Polish Jew and a Holocaust survivor who survived because of an underground resistance group. He and Nat became very close, and he offered Mark a position as an apprentice. It was a perfect fit. Mark was learning a new trade and making money. One day he came home with a motorcycle, not surprising for his thrill-seeking personality. I was clear, as long as he lived under my roof, he would not be driving a motorcycle. Mark reluctantly sold it back.

Eventually, we bought new furniture and fixed our home a little at a time. With the distractions of a busy life, time slipped by. Nat and I were not growing in our relationship. In fact, we had grown farther apart than ever.

Life Changes

I got a call from Paul Greenburg, a connection from the Rochelle Village Mall. He said, "The New Rochelle Mall is looking for a promotions director. Call them."

I interviewed with Bob Phelps and got the job. Finally, my days of drudgery in the insurance agency were over! I was doing the work I loved, and I reconnected with Selma Friedman.

New Rochelle Mall was run by Arlen Shopping Centers. It had its corporate headquarters in New York City and its shopping center division was headquartered in Chattanooga, Tennessee. Was it fate or chance that I would be connected to the city where my father and Natalie lived?

Those were the days of two martini lunches, standard for typical business meetings. Bob Phelps, my boss, was a two martini kind of guy. His indulgence had a marked effect on his work. When a group from the NYC branch arrived unexpectedly with clients and found Bob in a state that was not business appropriate, he was dismissed.

Eventually, CBL became the head of mall operations. My new boss, Ben Landris, was from Chattanooga, Tennessee. Once again, this New Yorker had a connection to Chattanooga. The search for a new mall manager began. A young black lawyer named Ron Johnson was hired. He was very bright but cautious and inexperienced. I helped him understand the "boots on the ground" aspects of mall management, and we became very close friends. All of these new changes were a wonderful opportunity for my personal growth. I learned a lot about how the larger corporate structure worked, and also, how adaptable and resilient I was.

As Bob Dylan said, "The times, they are a changin'." This was a time of racial discord in the United States. Many people had become afraid to shop at the New Rochelle Village Mall because of the race riots among blacks and whites, especially after the mall was looted during an uprising.

I became very active in the community and heard the term WASP for the first time. White Anglo-Saxon Protestant is an informal disparaging term for a small group of people whose family's connections and moneyed backgrounds allowed them access and connection to privilege not accessible to everyone. I was often the only Jew on many committees and boards. I didn't miss the irony when I was on the board of directors for the Salvation Army and rang the bell as I collected donations for Christmas. I also worked with the Catholic Church. I suppose I have always had a non-denominational heart when it comes to helping people.

I learned a lot about diversity, prejudice, tolerance and acceptance. I got to know the local newspaper editor, the on-air personalities at the local radio and television stations, and I learned how to rise above circumstance. I was able to make the challenging situation of a divided community a success when it came to shopping at our mall.

Mark graduated from high school and had to register for the draft. For as long as I could remember, someone in my family had been at war, from my relatives in World War I and World War II to Korea and now Vietnam. Mark had signed up for the National Guard fully expecting to go to Vietnam, but the day he was to report for duty, the war ended.

A traveling petting zoo came to the mall for the summer. There were lots of children's rides and an elephant, a donkey, giraffe and other animals that brought in the crowds. Both Stephen and Mark got jobs at the lowest level, which meant most of their time was spent shoveling manure and cleaning out pens. They made great money. Mark's future was uncertain; the only thing he knew for sure was that he did not want to go to college. He loved the characters that traveled with the zoo and decided this was better than working in the butcher

One of my presentations on events held at the New Rochelle Mall

shop. I spoke to the owner of the zoo, and he hired Mark to go on the road with them.

Mark was excited about a travel adventure only to return home after five days on the road. It seems he had hooked up with a group from the Ku Klux Klan. They all carried guns, and when they invited him to a meeting, they told him they had never met a Jew. He quickly realized this was not his future and was given a one-way train ticket home. He went back to work with Nat and Ludwig at the butcher shop on Saturdays.

Stephen was back at school struggling socially and academically. Nat and I were more roommates than husband and wife, both of us giving all we had to our jobs. While we had learned to avoid each other and avoid conflict, on Thanksgiving of nineteen-seventy-three, life changed.

This photo was taken in 2000 in front of 1320 Manor Avenue, the home in the Bronx where I lived until 1965.

On My Own

Just before Thanksgiving, Nat and I got into a heated dispute. Words flew. The pent up anger we both had for so many years erupted. I said, "I'm leaving!"

Nat said, "Get out! I'll be happy to take you somewhere else if you want to leave."

I packed my things in a big trunk and called his bluff. Nat drove me to an upstairs apartment of a home less than half a mile from our house where someone he knew had stayed. It was a small apartment owned by a couple called the Bongers. The place had a small living room, kitchen and a bedroom, all I needed. Little did Nat know I would really move out, especially on Thanksgiving.

I was forty years old and alone for the first time since I had left Mama Dora's home. I was a little depressed and feeling insecure, but all I could think was, "My God, I'm free!" I was embracing the idea of being away from Nat. Mark was twenty and Stephen was almost seventeen. They would be alright. I packed most of my personal belongings in a trunk and knew whatever might lie ahead, it would be better than the life I had been living. As unsettling as it was, I had no doubt it was the right thing for me to do. My landlords invited me to join them for Thanksgiving dinner, giving me a moment of comfort.

I returned to our house a few days later to pick up some things and Nat confronted me. He was angry; he never believed I would actually walk out. I stood my ground and felt the full fury of his rage as his huge hands reached around my neck. In a blind rage he began to squeeze until I almost passed out. If there was ever a doubt about my leaving, it vanished. That day I insisted, "I want a divorce!"

We hired Harold Gordon, the lawyer who had handled our auto accident case. He suggested counseling. I agreed so Nat could see that I would give him an option, but my heart was set on divorce. After a number of visits, individually and together, the counselor advised Nat just to let me go. Thankfully he did.

I told Nat he could have everything, the house, the furniture, the car, and our stocks. In those few weeks alone I was able to reflect on our marriage, and it thoroughly swept over me how long I had been miserable and how unfulfilled I was as a person. My sanity was at stake. I left with my used Vega and my next week's salary. No doubt the kids were in shock when they realized this was not a temporary situation. Of course, this would change their lives. The only comfort I had was that they were grown.

I loved both of my sons dearly but realized I could not go back to their father. I invited them to live with me, but they both chose to stay with Nat. Mark did not come to see me, but Stephen often came. He was very involved in wrestling and football at school. When his beloved Collie, Darren died, he came to me for comfort. Mark was still at the butcher shop and hung around with an offbeat group of kids. He was ready to move out and rented a house not far from home with three or four boys.

Nat had a girlfriend not long after I left. I stayed busy with work and loved my new found freedom. I was still vital and alive and realized that I enjoyed dating. Ironically, Nat and I would often see each other at local singles clubs, reminiscent of when we met so many years ago at the local social clubs. I think acceptance of our situation settled in, because we were polite to each other and would introduce our dates to each other.

New to the singles scene, I met a man named Joe Gerardi. The first time we danced, another fellow wanted to cut in. Joe wasn't willing to let me go and stood his ground. Things heated up and two grown men were having a fist fight because of me. I quickly left and heard from Joe soon after. He asked me for a date. I liked Joe. He was relaxed and comfortable to be around.

We had dated for about six or eight months when I went back to the club where we first met. I was startled to see Joe on the dance floor with a blond woman. I walked up behind him and said, "Hi Joe." He was surprised to see me and had no choice but to introduce me to his ex-wife. She seemed nice and wasn't threatened because I had already danced with Nat. It wasn't uncommon for divorced singles to have a variety of dance partners.

In the early hours of the morning, the phone woke me. It was Joe's wife. She told me she and Joe were getting back together, and she thanked me for the help I had given Joe to make it possible. I didn't know whether to laugh or cry. I realized that Nat and Joe had similar personalities.

Eventually, a woman named Miriam moved in with Nat. I didn't care what he did; I just wanted to be sure she treated the boys well. One day Stephen came to see me at the mall. He said, "Do you know Mark is selling dope?" I was stunned. I knew Mark had a wild streak, but I never expected this. I called Nat and asked if we could meet that evening.

Nat picked me up, and we went to Nathan's in Coney Island. Nat wanted to be sure that Miriam knew about our meeting because she would be jealous. When I asked if he knew Mark was selling dope, I was taken aback when he said yes. He said that Miriam knew "the boys" and that they were looking out for Mark. In New York, the expression, "the boys" always meant mafia ties.

I was shocked to know that Nat was condoning these deals. Mark was living away from home with friends and not working. He would not talk to me. I was deeply concerned and didn't know where to turn. My anger and frustration were apparent.

Nat drove me home, and I asked him if he wanted to come in for a few minutes. I was still very disturbed about Mark, and I needed some kind of resolution or plan of action. All I could think about was what a dangerous road Mark had chosen.

Out of nowhere Nat grabbed me and wanted to kiss me. I shouted, "Stop it, Nat! No, stop it!!"

All of his six-foot-two, two-hundred and fifty pounds was on top of me as he threw me on the bed and raped me. He tossed me aside and went back home to Miriam. I knew that would be the last time I would ever trust him. He had injured my soul in a way that was unforgivable. I had always known it was the right decision to leave. This combined with Nat condoning Mark's behavior confirmed my resolution to make it on my own. Our divorce was final in June of 1974. Nat's father, Harry, said to him, "You should have taken the Cadillac." This was a bitter reminder that he had offered Nat a Cadillac if he would not marry me.

Determined to Survive

Women's rights had come a long way, but the glass ceiling was ever present. It was a political term used to describe both gender and the minority inequality in the workplace. Regardless of my experience and willingness to work hard in every area of my field, it was impossible to make it to the top of the corporation. The lead management jobs were always given to men.

I needed a life change. I took a job at the Mid-Island Fashion Plaza in Hicksville, New York, because it was different and also, close to home. Christmas was approaching and the mall needed a Santa. After many interviews, I chose a black man because he was the most qualified. My boss said, "Get rid of him, or you are fired!" I was disgusted to have to tell him I could not give him a job. I hired a fat woman; it was my only way to retaliate without losing my job. My position at Mid-Island was short lived because I couldn't tolerate the manager. As it happened, the person who had taken my place at the New Rochelle Mall wasn't working out, and they wanted me back.

I was still living at the Bongers. In fact, I would spend the next two years there. What a curious family! Otto Bongers' brother had been in Hitler's army, strange for a Jew to hear. But that was the least of what was weird about the Bongers. Otto Bonger had a reputation for being off the wall. Otto kept a pet alligator named Irving that he raised from a small gator in the house. He was forced to give it to the zoo because of its size, not to mention the fear it instilled in the neighbors. Thankfully the gator was sent to the zoo just before I moved in. He also had a pet crow that lived in the house. He had found it with a broken wing and nursed it back to health.

Madeline Bonger, his wife, was a Blackfoot Indian, originally from Montreal, Canada. She spoke fluent French and had an open and friendly disposition. She was always inviting me to dinner and welcomed me as part of their family. They had two daughters and two sons who came with husbands, boyfriends and friends. Together, they were a unique, quirky and diverse group of people.

All of their children were very close to their parents. Their daughter, Carole, lived at home and was a sergeant in the Army. Carole was a lesbian, a shocking admission at that time in history, especially as part of the military. One of their sons was a policeman who frequently cheated on his wife knowing his mother would provide an alibi and condone his behavior. Their second son was a mama's boy who came home for a home cooked meal every day.

Living there brought back memories of living with Mama Dora at Manor Avenue and our apartment house always filled with curious tenants. However odd, I was thankful for a make-do family. Fifteen years later I would find the Bongers back in my life when I moved to Chattanooga, Tennessee. In Fact, I have stayed in touch with members of that family throughout my life.

Fate or Coincidence?

Ben Landris, my boss, said, "Moes Lebovitz will be here Saturday with his wife. I need you to be here to show him around." Moes Lebovitz just happened to be from Chattanooga. As I was showing them around the mall, he kept asking me personal questions. He asked me if my father was Jack Jamieson. At that time, I had no idea that my father had met Moes at Ben Zion Synagogue in Chattanooga.

My father had said to Moes, "Do you know my daughter, Roslynne, works for you at the New Rochelle Mall?

Moes returned to Chattanooga and told my father that I was attractive and competent. For the first time in my life, after forty years, my father recognized that I had worth.

I had to go to a seminar in Augusta, Georgia. It was a bizarre experience to see the Ku Klux Klan on the march and realize this was a reality in the Deep South. I never imagined myself living in the South. After the seminar, I traveled to Chattanooga to visit my father and Natalie. He could not wait to take me to the synagogue on Saturday morning. After service, Moes and his wife came up and gave me a big hug. My father was so proud of me. What a life change! When I was first divorced, my father blamed me. After this visit, our relationship took a hundred and eighty degree turn. I headed back to New York with a new hope for my future. It is too bad that it took one of Chattanooga's leading citizens to open my father's eyes, but I thank you, Moes Lebovitz – May you rest in peace!

It is uncanny how the threads of life reappear. Maybe it is just unfinished business resurfacing when I am ready to handle it. I was talking to a mall manager from Long Island, who was a close friend of Ray Heatherton. I shared the story about what a profound difference his generosity had made in

Donald's life as he faced his last days in the hospital. I asked if Ray and his wife would visit the mall. Ray arrived and hugged me like we were long-lost friends. It was a very successful promotion with huge crowds and great press coverage. I was grateful for the smallest opportunity to promote Ray after all he had done for Donald.

ADVANCE PLANNING

THE MALL IN NEW ROCHELLE HOSTS EASTER SEAL TELETHON

THE MALL IN NEW ROCHELLE, NEW YORK HOSTED THE WESTCHESTER EASTER SEAL TELETHON ON MARCH 27th & 28th. THERE WERE OVER TWO HUNDRED VOLUNTEERS FROM ORGANIZATIONS, COLLEGES AND YOUTH GROUPS TO ANSWER PHONES FOR THE TWENTY HOUR PERIOD. PEOPLE STOPPING BY THE MALL WERE ALSO ENTERTAINED. THE FESTIVITIES STARTED SATURDAY AT 10:00 PM WHEN WESTCHESTER ROCKLAND NEWSPAPERS VICE PRESIDENT MARK ARNOLD AND HIS BAND PER-FORMED. MUSIC CONTINUED WITH A VARIETY OF GROUPS THROUGH SUNDAY. THERE WAS RADIO & NEWSPAPER PUBLICITY BOTH LOCAL AND COUNTY-WIDE, ALSO VIDEO TAPES WERE PRODUCED BY THE WESTCHESTER ON THE SOUND JUNIOR LEAGUE WHICH WERE SHOWN ON WPIX, CHANNEL 11. MALL MERCHANTS DONATED FOOD & EQUIPMENT FOR THE VOLUNTEERS. OVER $16,000. WAS COLLECTED FROM WESTCHESTER COUNTY ALONE.

Roslynne Steinberg
Promotion Director

NATIONAL RESEARCH BUREAU, INC.

Another Change

I was doing my best at New Rochelle Mall going to as many career seminars and personal growth opportunities as I was able to. Opportunities were limited for women to move up the corporate ladder at that time. I was offered a job by Buddy Zarrett, the vice president of Photo Promotion Associates, located in Monsey, New York.

I accepted the position of marketing director for the shopping center and military accounts. It was an opportunity for personal growth and a welcome change. They were a fast growing organization with lots of flash and money. I would have a lot of opportunities to travel to many of the big malls in the United States. They were also in direct competition with Olan Mills, with its headquarters in Chattanooga, Tennessee.

The excellent salary, fast-paced business, opportunity to travel and meet new people was just what I needed. The company paid for me to move about fifty miles away. I took all I owned and moved lock, stock and barrel to upstate New York at the foot of the Catskill Mountains. I was excited to be making a change and testing myself as I stepped away from all that was familiar to me. I found an apartment in the upstairs part of an enormous, hundred-year-old home in Pearl River, New York, on the banks of the Hudson.

I leaped into learning an entirely new career and was booking Photo Promotion Associates into malls throughout the United States. I had a grand adventure. I was learning a new trade and loving the challenge. "Wagman the Bagman," as he was called, was the company president. He had done jail time for fixing games. I was still young and naïve, having no idea how unethical behavior by the company president might affect our future.

In those days "headliners" or celebrity figures were a popular way to gather crowds at mall events. George, better known as "Georgie" Jessel was one of Buddy's best friends. He was born in the Bronx and was a well-known actor, singer, songwriter, and movie producer. He became famous for being a comedic entertainer and was often asked to serve as the master of ceremonies at entertainment and political gatherings. He served at so many functions he became known as, "the toastmaster general of the United States." He had an engraved walking stick that he said was given to him by President Truman.

Georgie Jessel was the celebrity figure chosen to support Photo Promotions. We spent a great deal of time traveling around the country together, always in style. My job was to book the events, create press opportunities and make sure Mr. Jessel was ready to show up as a guest for the events. I was in my forties, and he was in his eighties when we met. It was an eye-opening lesson for me to see how quickly the fame can fade. I knew I wanted to become a deeper and wiser human being as I aged, and I wanted to be more than just a polished veneer of my former self. My time working with George Jessel confirmed the realization that I had so long ago in the Borsch Belt of the Catskills when Nat and I were first married. I never wanted to look back at my life and say, "I would have, could have, and should have." I was going to be a master of my fate.

Georgie Jessel lived in Hollywood, California. We often did trade shows, and he always made a guest appearance. Part of my responsibility was to book a hotel and make sure we had the best suite available, often the penthouse, and to ensure the events went off without a hitch. We had flamboyant parties, excellent food, and the alcohol flowed like water. Guests came in and out at all hours. It was a great way to introduce Photo Promotions, and the company was growing, fast.

It was all part of the business as we traveled to and from New Orleans, Chicago, Phoenix, Las Vegas, Atlanta and other locations around the country. We even visited Toronto. Working in malls meant I needed to stay in touch with all the latest fashion, and I dressed the part. Stockings and heels were par for the course, although walking through huge malls on hard concrete floors left my feet and legs exhausted by the end of the week. As the public relations person, my role was to be in touch will all the shopping center managers and make sure the events ran smoothly. Malls were relatively new but springing up at lightning speed around the country.

Photo Promotions always wanted to be showy. We had two company limousines, and sometimes Georgie Jessel and I would be driven to events together. Georgie was an alcoholic, and his drinking becoming heavier by the day as he realized his time in Hollywood was over, and international trade shows were the best gig he had. Photo Promotions paid him very well, and he always stayed in the presidential suite or the penthouse.

I set up *four*, eighty-one-year-old birthday celebrations for Georgie! I would order a fabulous birthday cake, food, and drinks, as an opportunity to entertain chain store CEOs. I always made promotional arrangements in advance of our arrival. As I made special arrangements for another eighty-first birthday party in one of Toronto's finest hotels, many press releases were sent to local and major television media. This was a huge shopping event, with a large attendance of store owners expected. Two hours before the big birthday bash, I discovered there was no birthday cake! I called management only to find that the chef knew nothing about a birthday party for Georgie Jessel. I told them there would be lots of media coverage, and this oversight would look awful for the hotel. Five minutes later I got a call back saying the cake would be on time. Good thing, because the next morning the event was broadcast on television. It was just another day at the "office".

Georgie was as bald as a cue ball and refused to go out without his toupee that looked like a cheap polyester rug. In the morning from his private room that was across the spacious, well-appointed luxury suite, I would hear him call, "Rose, I need a Jack and Coke." For some reason, he never could say Roslynne. Even before he put his dentures in he was ready to start the morning with a drink. He stayed in bed most of the day propped up on pillows. With his silk robe and whiskey in hand, he entertained guests and spent the rest of the day on the phone with his agent. He bemoaned his fate at playing second fiddle to the great entertainers of the day. He told me stories about Jerry Lewis and Frank Sinatra and other stars he knew.

When it was time to head down to the mall for the event, or when guests were expected in the suite, I would lay out his clothes. One day Regis Philbin and associates stopped by. Regis said, "What a horrible toupée! I'll send you a good one when I get back to the city." When we returned to New York, sure enough, there were two quality wigs waiting for him.

Georgie loved young women, and they often came up to the hotel suite to visit. His stay in bed lying around in a bathrobe was meant to have the same swagger as Hugh Hefner; it didn't translate the same way. A young lady from Germany came up to meet the toastmaster general of the United States as he was often referred to. As she got near his bed, he grabbed her and pulled her towards him.

She quickly pulled away, tidying her clothes and saying, "Frisky isn't he?"

I pushed him to events in his wheelchair and could hear young people whisper, "How's the corpse?" His heyday had come and gone, but he was holding on to the dream of Hollywood success. I thought it would be fun to have a buxom blonde in a nurse's uniform wheel him around, but no one took me up on that idea.

From Boys to Men

Back at home, Mark was still selling dope as a middle-man. Sadly, many of his friends were his customers, and they did not pay him. He was a better salesman than a collection agent. He finally left the drug trade and bought a kosher butcher shop in the Forest Hills area of Queens. He was twenty-one and thrilled to own his butcher shop. I came down from Pearl River to help out as a cashier on Sundays. Nat and his father, Harry, also helped out part-time. What a relief to see Mark on a straight path!

Mark and his father counting receipts from the grand opening of Mark's butcher shop, Steinberg's Kosher Meats, on Queens Boulevard

Stephen was ready to graduate from Elmont High School. Some of his best friends got accepted at the Maine Maritime Academy in Castine, Hancock County, Maine. Stephen got a football scholarship there and headed off to pursue a degree in Marine Engineering. He was just one of two Jewish boys at

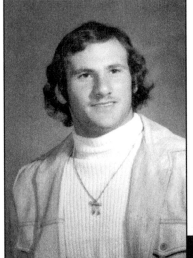

Stephen as a graduate of Elmont High School.

the school. He seemed happy. Shortly after the first season, he injured his knees and was unable to play football, so he became an assistant football coach. He stayed for four years, and this journey set the course for a lifetime career path.

Stephen in uniform at the Marine Maritime Academy in Castine, Maine

The Dark Side of Big Business

I was happy my boys were doing so well and knew I had to find my way. Hard work was what I knew how to do. One day I got a call from Frank McGuire who was a retired businessman making money under the table, which he referred to as a "special arrangement." He was a wheeler-dealer who could always sniff out an excellent opportunity. He had an in with a big chain store operation, and he thought that he could arrange for all of these stores to feature Photo Promotions.

I brought his proposal to the company president and set up a meeting for him to meet Aaron Wagman. Aaron liked the deal, and he flew me to Tampa, Florida, to get the contract signed. I carried a money belt under my clothes containing $10,000 in cash and feeling like I was a drug mule. I didn't ask any questions; I figured it was just part of the deal.

Time passed, and I began to realize that big business had its drawbacks. Buddy Zarrett, Vice President of Photo Promotions, was the only decent officer in the company. He was the one who hired me and was like a son to Georgie Jessel. Aside from Buddy Zarrett, business life seemed to be full of immorality. Or maybe it always had been immoral, and I just began to notice. A lot of underhanded things were going on, and this was becoming a job that I no longer felt comfortable doing.

The best part of my work was my secretary. Rita Albert became a close confidant and a dear friend. She was wise and well aware how tough business can be. Rita helped me navigate many challenging circumstances.

Frank McGuire was impressed with me because I was making money for the company. One day I approached him with an idea that I thought would increase the business profits. I suggested that when we sent back the family proofs after their portraits were taken, that we also send a brochure filled

Cash In On
America's
Jazziest Numbers!

See Rozmo. This was a Photo Promtions ad for the 1980 trade show in New Orleans

with novelties along with frames and shelves to display customer's portraits. Frank loved the idea and saw the addition of a novelty catalog as a way to open the world of financial potential. The catalog took off.

Frank decided to make me Vice President of the corporation and give me shares of stock in the company. I was both thrilled and naïve to think that my promotion would be accepted across the board.

Two of the partners, Aaron Wagman, and Mike Weber wanted me out. My idea was making the company money, but everyone did not want to share the rewards. They offered to buy my shares for two-thousand four-hundred dollars. I refused because I felt bullied, and I wanted to share the long-term benefits.

Life became increasingly unpleasant for me at work. There was a large theft in the office, and we were all forced to submit to a lie detector test from a bonding company. The thief turned out to be a teenager with a drug addiction that one of the partners was sleeping with. As the layers of corruption in this company were peeled back, I knew I needed to get out. I was in a no-win situation, but I couldn't afford to quit.

Most of my time was devoted to working, but on occasion, I dated. I never met anyone I wanted to marry. During my time at Photo Promotions, I had a long distance fling with Jack Frost, the Detroit regional manager. We always got together at trade shows. As situations changed, the President of Photo Promotions had Jack call and threaten me.

I knew Jack was a coward, especially to behave that way towards me. I told him that he didn't scare me one bit. I reminded him that when he met my sons at our company Christmas party he said he was afraid of them because they kept staring at him. I didn't hesitate to tell him that if anything happened to me, they would beat the living shit out of him. That feisty girl in me from my early days in the Bronx never left.

I was in my forties, and I was already beginning to feel old in a

At the 1980 trade show in New Orleans

In Halloween costume for Photo Promotion Associates

business driven by youth. I had bags under my eyes and decided plastic surgery would help me look younger and feel better about myself. Plastic surgery was nowhere near as advanced as it is today, and the risks were much greater. However, I felt like it was necessary to compete in a very social industry.

One day as I was leaving work wearing the dark glasses required for surgery, a couple of men were coming my way waving. One said, "Are you Roslynne? We'd like to talk to you."

He was the president of a company called Heirloom Portraits, a subsidiary of Kiddie Kolor, a business from Flushing, New York, that specialized in heirloom portraits. They had been watching Photo Promotions and wanted to grow their business in a similar way. They thought I was just the person to get the job done and offered me a job. The timing was perfect, and once again I stepped into an unknown future. I accepted their offer. They paid for my move to Flushing, New York, a borough of Queens.

Stephen

Just before I moved to Queens, Stephen came to visit. He brought an attractive young lady, Angela DeGiglio, with him. She was a charming and sweet Italian girl who had just graduated from nursing school. Stephen was ready to graduate from the Marine Maritime Academy, and he was part of a crew that had taken a cruise ship to Bermuda.

As fate would have it, Angela was in Bermuda celebrating her graduation with a group of nurses from New York. The attraction between Angela and Stephen was instant. Angela promised Stephen that she would meet him during The Parade of Ships. This was an event that he would be participating in to celebrate the maritime history in the United States. It is held annually on the Hudson River and in New York Harbor. Angela was there, as promised, and a lifetime romance began.

Stephen graduated and moved back in with Nat at Valley Stream. The place was a roach infested disaster, so Stephen came to live with me. He had hoped to get a job on a tanker, but at that time most of the oil shipping lines were owned and operated by Arab countries, and they were hesitant to hire Jews. He found a job with Sun Oil, an American company, as a maritime engineer.

Within a year, he and Angela were engaged. Angela was from an Italian Catholic family who moved to the United States when she was twelve. Harry, Stephen's grandfather, was not happy that Stephen chose to marry outside of his faith. They had a beautiful wedding honoring both their Jewish and Catholic faiths.

On February 12, 1983, Stephen was serving as a maritime engineer aboard the SS Tropic Sun. He was on watch that evening when a distress call came in from the SS Marine Electric, a coast guard tanker en route from Virginia to Massachusetts. They had encountered a massive storm and sank in the icy waters. Only three of the thirty-four crew members survived. Stephen pulled many of the frozen dead bodies from the water that night. He still has nightmares. This disaster brought about safety changes in the Coast Guard's marine inspection program, including the Coast Guard rescue swimmer program.

Kiddie Kolor

I immersed myself in my new job. Kiddie Kolor thought supermarkets would be a potential market, so I set out to use my collective experience and build accounts.

My first store was in Harlem. At that time, civil rights issues and segregation were in turmoil across the country. Harlem was predominately black and an explosively dangerous neighborhood filled with drugs and crime. I was the only white face anywhere in the area, and I was uneasy about approaching that first supermarket. Fortunately, I found a parking spot just outside.

In those days, I always dressed up. It was part of the business, and I loved fashion. I was wearing a blue suede knee length coat, heels and diamond rings, not typical dress for grocery shopping at that store. A police car was parked nearby. I approached the officers and said I had a business appointment and asked if they would keep an eye out for me. Their advice was to turn my rings around and walk with confidence. Refusing to be intimidated, I steadied myself and sealed the deal.

During my time at Kiddie Kolor, I also sought out business from military bases and malls, as I had done at Photo Promotions. I did not have a no compete contract. However, as soon as Photo Promotions became aware that I was in what they perceived to be their territory, they threatened to sue me for five million dollars. They sent me a summons, and my boss got one as well. He said not to worry; he would handle things. Thankfully nothing ever came of it. That was another business lesson I learned from.

I soon realized that Kiddie Kolor did not have a solid foundation, and I was in a dead-end job. They were short of sales people and new ideas, which added up to limited growth potential. I continued to stay in touch with people in the marketing industry, and I had heard through the grapevine that my former position as marketing director for New Rochelle Mall was open.

Back at the Mall

A new shopping center management company, Aries Brandenburg, had taken over. I had a good reputation and still knew many of the merchants I had worked with in the past, so for the third time, I found myself back at New Rochelle Mall.

BRONX NEWS — THURSDAY, JULY 15, 1982 - 21

INSIDE THE MALL

BY ROSYLNNE STEINBERG

Sidewalk Sale

By Roslynne Steinberg
Since 1972, the New Rochelle Mall have pleased their customers by presenting Sidewalk Sales. The merchants will bring tables and racks loaded with merchandise out into the Mall. It will look like an old fashioned market place from the 20's. The values are fantastic and many merchants have cut prices 50% and below cost.

The date for this rock bottom price event is July 15-18 (Thursday-Sunday).

The merchants and employees of the mall have been encouraged to dress according to the 1920's era. You will be welcomed by flappers and dappers, also there will be strolling entertainment. Not only will there be an atmosphere of festivity throughout the Mall, but inflation fighting prices to boot. Don't miss it. See the ad for mall hours and directions.

Another column promoting the New Rochelle Mall in 1982.

Things did not go as anticipated. I had been the marketing director for less than six months when they fired me. I was in my late forties and traded in for a "younger model." I was angry and indignant. I knew I was doing a good job and that I had a solid relationship with the mall merchants, many of whom I had kept in touch with during the years I was away from the mall. Not only was merchant satisfaction high, but I was also doing a lot of publicity that was bringing in the crowds. I believed I lost my job because they wanted someone younger.

My dear friend and former secretary at Photo Promotions, Rita Albert, also knew Photo Promotions was a dead end job. Rita had moved to Queens and found a job at a big barter company in New York City. She knew a lawyer from the National Organization for Women, and she set up a meeting. The lawyer felt my concerns had merit and suggested I go to the Civil Liberties Union. The Civil Liberties Union sent a subpoena to Aries Brandenburg on my behalf.

In the meantime, Aries Brandenburg let the young girl go that they had hired in my place. To my surprise and delight, they hired my old friend and mentor, Selma Friedman, with whom I had remained in touch throughout the years. Eventually, the lawsuit was dropped for "lack of evidence."

In a twist of justice, while Selma was working for Aries Brandenburg, something fell on her, and she filed a lawsuit against the company and was awarded ten thousand dollars. Her keen sense of justice and willingness to stand up for what she believed continued to inspire me. Selma and I remained friends until her death almost forty years later.

New Career

I decided it was time to find a new career. Thankfully, I was able to collect unemployment while I searched for what would become my next profession. Century 21 Best placed an ad in the paper seeking real estate agents, "no experience necessary." I thought real estate would be a good match for my skills and love of people, and I knew there would be no age barrier selling real estate. I got the job! The New York real estate laws were difficult, and I studied diligently so I could get my license and begin to solicit listings. I passed the local and state exams and became a licensed agent with a Century 21 Gold Jacket.

Time was of the essence. There was a lengthy training period with no pay until I made my first commission. I knew my unemployment would not last forever. It was 1984. I was fifty-one years old and on my own. It was "do or die." I was not happy just to do, and I sure as hell didn't plan to die. I wanted to be the best, and I thought this would be my last chance to make enough money to secure my financial future.

What a career! There were over forty agents in the company, stiff competition! I believed the adage, "The early bird gets the worm." I was up early and in bed late, investing all of my energy into learning the world of real estate. My first experience using a computer and deciphering multiple listings was another challenge. There were no cell phones in those days – we all had beepers. I drove the streets looking for listings. I spent a lot of time canvassing neighborhoods and making cold calls. "For sale by owner" signs were a perfect opportunity to offer my services.

That approach had its issues. I walked up to a door and with startling speed two huge, threatening Doberman Pinchers darted out of nowhere. I barely dodged their snarling fangs as I quickly became aware of unexpected job hazards.

Each agent had a territory. Mine was made up of many foreigners. I had clients who were Chinese, Japanese, Indian and Russian. When it came time to talk money, I don't know how I pulled it off, but somehow we worked through the language barriers, and I began making sales.

A Business Partner

Upon meeting one of our new agents, Joshua Kramer. I was impressed with his accomplishments. His family had come from Israel to Sioux City, Iowa, where his father became a *shochet*. A *shochet* is a rabbi trained to kill animals with compassion so they may be considered as kosher food. Josh's strict upbringing certainly didn't match his showy personality and his gay lifestyle. He was always wanting bigger and better and was in hot pursuit of making money to fund his way of life. I admired his ambition.

Joshua had come to New York to attend school where he graduated from Yeshiva University. Later he studied interior decorating at Fashion Institute of Technology, quite a change from farm life in Iowa. He had a great personality and a fantastic sense of humor. He was a year younger than my son Stephen, and I took him under my wing.

We began to canvass territories together as sales agents. If our listings sold, we shared the money. We did very well as partners and became great friends in the process. I may have been a few decades older, but we were a good match because of our drive and ambition and desire to make a lot of money.

After a long week of selling real-estate, we needed to unwind. Gail Green was an agent in our office. She was very sophisticated with a sarcastic sense of humor. Gail always liked to be thought of as the top salesperson, and the best at whatever she did. When she walked in the room, tall and thin with long painted nails, she looked as if she could be a fashion model. Gail lived in a well-to-do area of town with a much older man, Henry, who was a German Jew. She was an alcoholic, and I had heard rumors that her behavior could get out of hand when she was drunk, but so far I hadn't seen it. Along with Henry, she had a young boyfriend, Steve.

Many evenings after work Gail, Steve, Josh and I would go out for drinks. After nearly a year at Century 21 Best, Gail asked me if I was interested in going into business with her. I had an uneasy feeling I couldn't identify, so trusting my instincts, I declined. Josh and I continued to work well together as a team, and I felt like we had an excellent relationship.

Josh and I got some inside information about a Trump apartment complex in Rego Park that was going to become a co-op complex. Real estate tycoon Fred Trump owned the apartment complex. Fred was well known in the real estate world long before his son, Donald Trump, became a household name as a real estate mogul.

At that time, the laws allowed you to buy a co-op if you already lived there before they transitioned from apartments into co-ops. Co-ops were a good investment because they could bring a much higher price than an apartment. Josh rented an apartment intending to buy while it was still available at an apartment price. I agreed to move in because we could see the potential windfall when they turned to co-ops.

I moved in only to find myself in the worst roach infested place I had ever lived. The first night I woke up to find myself crawling with cockroaches! It was a nightmare right out of a Hitchcock movie. I called Josh hysterical, screaming, "I've had enough, and I can't do this!"

He said, "Calm down and start counting those roaches. Think of them as cash, and you'll see how much money we'll make." I was just as hungry as Josh was to make a lot of money, and he sure knew how to motivate me. After using hundreds of roach motels and professional extermination treatments, along with many sleepless nights, I agreed to stay because of the potential profit.

Using "insider information" was illegal. A close watch was kept on professional real estate agents. When Josh went to close on the apartment, he found himself summoned to court because he was not living in the apartment, a legal requirement. I was implicated because I had moved in so we could make a quick profit. Even though we knew many real estate lawyers, it was clear we were in trouble.

We were worried about our future. We had no idea how we could get out of this mess without losing our licenses. I came up with the idea that we should claim I was Josh's girlfriend, and he was keeping me. A stretch, since I was twice his age. Our lawyer laughed but agreed. The regulators believed us, and we bought an apartment for fifteen thousand dollars, shortly after they turned into co-ops. A year later we sold it for forty-five thousand, making a hefty profit while giving me a fabulous place to live for a year.

I was out of an apartment, but we were high on our success! When Josh found out that the apartment building that he lived in would also be turned into condos, he suggested that we should invest there and that I should move in. He had heard that a place on the twelfth floor was for sale. Although tenants had the first option to buy, Josh lived in the penthouse on the thirteenth floor, so he knew the potential. He used his position as a board member of the tenant's association to ensure I was accepted as the new tenant.

The building was in Kew Gardens on the corner of Main and Queens Boulevard. The views were spectacular. At night from the outside terrace, I could see the Whitestone Bridge, a suspension bridge that crosses the East River and connects Queens on Long Island and the Bronx. I saw the Throggs Neck Bridge that connects the East River and Long Island Sound. Lights danced across the Triborough Bridge that spans the Harlem River, the Bronx, and part of the East River. This prime location with extraordinary views also had a parking garage, which was a rarity in the city, and it had a doorman.

We learned from the first purchase of an apartment going co-op that we needed to be above board this time. We knew the tenants that were moving, and we offered them fifteen thousand dollars for the furniture and carpeting they left behind, which they accepted. When the units became condos, I took out a mortgage for a hundred and eighty thousand, bought in, and was living like a queen. No doubt the place is worth five hundred thousand, or more, today.

There was a massive influx of Russian Jews coming to the United States for religious freedom. They moved to Brighton Beach, Brooklyn, which became known as "Little Odessa." A Russian couple came to the office with their father. They worked selling hot dogs from a pushcart on the street corners in Manhattan. It reminded me of my early days at 1320 Manor Avenue when push carts were common. I thought of my Russian heritage on my mother's side of the family.

When they came to see me, the language barrier was challenging. They would extend their hands and say, "Cash, cash; we have cash." I understood they wanted to move out of their apartment and buy their first home. They worked long hours on the streets, so the only time I could meet them at their apartment was before dawn, late night, or Sunday.

One Sunday afternoon I was at their place, and we were working out the details of a home they had decided to purchase. I was sitting in a beautifully carved upholstered chair, one of their finer possessions. I was in my early fifties at the time and approaching menopause. At times, this situation caused unexpected, heavy bleeding. We were wrapping up the details, and as I rose to leave, I felt a sudden gush of fluid run down my thigh. To my great embarrassment, I realized I had left a deep crimson stain on their upholstered chair, as well as my clothes! The woman of the house was kind enough to offer me some assistance and clean clothes. As I emerged from the bathroom wearing borrowed clothes, I had to face the men.

Being Russian, they were all gathered together drinking vodka. At least the legwork was done, and we were ready to seal the deal. No amount of embarrassment was going to cause me to lose my sale. I maintained my dignity and tried to make a gracious exit. I smiled as I said, "Gentlemen, I'll be in touch."

They next day, back at the office, I was shocked to see my fellow agent, Nilo Delatorre sitting with my Russian clients. It was obvious he was negotiating a deal. I didn't know if the incident at their home was a contributing factor, but I knew as an agent we were expected to respect each other's territories and business, especially when a deal was in the works!

I went into Bernie Weiss' office. He was our lead broker and owner-manager. I asked him if Nilo was taking an offer on the house I had just talked about at our weekly meeting, and he said, "Yes, he is."

I was pissed! It was obvious that Bernie was not going to intervene on my behalf, so I took matters into my hands. I let Nilo complete the deal. When the clients left, I asked to speak to Nilo in private. I said, "You know I have been working with these clients, and I was ready to get a binder when I had an accident and had to leave their home unexpectedly. This is clearly my commission, but I am willing to give you half." I conceded half because I didn't know if my accident and ruining their chair (even though I had offered to have it cleaned) had offended them.

Nilo shook his head and said, "No way."

I was so angry at the injustice and his unethical behavior that I leaned in and whispered, "Nilo, you will give me half of the commission, or I will cut your fucking balls off!"

Nilo was stunned but quickly backed off as he said, "Oh… okay."

I have no doubt that he realized I should have had a hundred percent of the commission and that I meant business. We split the commission and remained friends. Even though he was almost twenty years younger, he tried to make a move on me shortly after this incident.

Successful Partnership

Josh Kramer and I were great partners, and we were making money. While we were still at Century 21 Best, we decided to go into business for ourselves and open our own office. It was a significant decision. Josh and I had worked together for about a year, and during that time, we had developed a deep level of trust and respect for one another. He appreciated all of my sales experience and respected my confidence. I thought he was smart and capable and would be a great partner.

Our first step, in setting up our firm, was to get our brokers licenses. It was a legal requirement to have the general manager we were working for to endorse us. Bernie Weiss was happy to do that for us. After our broker's licenses, we needed a real estate office just to get started. We would need a lot of capital, but we believed in ourselves, and we were tired of giving so much of our hard earned commissions to someone else.

I studied hard at St. John's University and earned my broker's license in 1985. The law required that each Century 21 company be a certain distance from another to provide an equal opportunity for real estate agents. We found a storefront on Corona Avenue in Elmhurst Queens, a neighborhood formerly known for its Italian population. It was rapidly becoming an area more like the United Nations. There was a mix of Europeans, Latinos, Chinese and Koreans. It seemed that most of the sellers were American and the buyers were foreign.

Bob Cassandra owned the building. He owned an oil company along with a lot of prime property on Corona Avenue in Queens. He was well known in the Italian community for his business savvy. When we met Bob, he was very well dressed and had a lot of swagger. His two brothers were at the meeting. Unlike Bob, they looked like a pair of muscled, grizzly, street fighters. Bob was impressed with us, and I sold him on the idea of renovating and renting us the first floor of the building as a real-estate office. We promised to keep an eye out for available properties and appealing business opportunities where Bob could invest.

Now that we had the space we had to raise the money to open. I had saved my money and had ten thousand dollars to invest. Josh sold his Manhattan condo for his share of the investment making us fifty-fifty partners. Rita Albert, my former secretary, and longtime friend, who had also become a real estate agent at Century 21 Best, invested ten thousand dollars as a silent partner. We had also made some successful investments on handy-man specials that gave us much-needed operating capital. We hired Rita's brother, Mel Feldman, to set up our books.

We signed a contract and were ready to celebrate! We were so excited that we decided to invite our friends Gail and Steve to join us at an uptown restaurant. We didn't tell them why; we wanted to wait and personally share our great plans. We sat down and proposed a toast as we broke the news.

To my absolute astonishment, Gail turned to Josh and said, "This is gross! Why in the hell are you going into business with this old cunt?"

I couldn't believe my ears! I was completely dumbfounded. When I regained my composure, I lashed out in anger as I said, "Well, let me tell you, some of the agents in the office say you look just like a transvestite!"

Josh and Steve were both shocked by this sudden turn of events. Their fear was evident when they saw the look on Gail's face. She had transformed from a drunken insulting woman into a lunatic with a look of murderous rage. She rose from her chair, her face red as a beet, as she hissed at me clawing her long fingers right in my face. I thought she was going to claw my eyes out!

As she leaned over the table, she grabbed a bottle of red wine and came at me. Just as I thought she was going to hit me with it, with a flip of her wrist, she began to pour it over my head! All eyes were on us, and the waiters jumped to attention. A waiter immediately escorted her out of the restaurant with Steve following close behind.

Josh shook with fear! The waiters brought me stacks of napkins, and I wiped myself off. I was shocked and angry. Josh was afraid that Gail was hiding in the parking lot waiting to ambush us. As I drove, he kept turning around to see if we were being followed. I kept an eye on the rearview mirror all the way home. If ever there was a confirmation that we had made a good decision to leave the company, this was it!

The next day Josh and I informed Century 21 Best of our decision. Real estate was a "dog-eat-dog" world, and they were surprised to learn we would now be their competitors. Some of our former friends quickly became our enemies. Our Century 21 franchise opened on Corona Avenue in Elmhurst, Queens. We called it Century 21 Elms. We hired Steve Weisel, a real-estate broker from Century 21 Best, to train and manage our agents. We interviewed and hired half-a-dozen agents; a few came with us from Century 21 Best. We were on our way!

Shortly after our move, Metropolitan Life bought all of the Century 21 franchises, presenting a new opportunity. If I also became an insurance broker, we would be entitled to a referral fee from any clients who bought a home, auto, and life insurance. The exams were difficult, but I took them, and that allowed me to refer Metropolitan Life insurance to our clients. Of Course, all of the fees and commissions went right back to the business.

Josh and I were working seven days a week from dawn to midnight. We divided our talents. I had advertising experience, so I handled all of the print and radio media. We were accruing overhead at a fast pace, so we needed cash. Josh was on the lookout for any and all properties. By now, Steve Weisel had recruited and trained about forty agents. We had an army of Gold Jackets. Owning our own business, was never dull!

Our best deals came when we could buy houses all cash – something our landlord, Bob Cassandra, was rolling in. Bob would lend us the money at twenty percent interest to be paid back in a year. We were able to turn most of our properties over in six months.

A Haitian client asked me to list his house in a rough area of Jamaica Queens. The house was listed for more than a year. Just when we were ready to take it off the market, it burned to the ground. The brick house frame covered in ash and our lone real estate sign was all that remained. Just when we were sure that the listing was dead, some Rastafarians offered us seventy thousand dollars in cash! Most of it was in five and ten dollar bills, with a lot of ones. It took us two days to count the money. We asked no questions and attorneys were present to keep this honest. Even though the commission was only four thousand dollars, we were thankful to have much-needed cash.

A Jewish Synagogue was just across the street from our office. I had a good relationship with the board of directors, so when they decided to sell, they asked us to be their agent. We found a buyer making us both listing and selling agent. A Pentecostal church bought the building for four hundred thousand dollars, giving us a windfall of forty thousand dollars.

But soon our luck of changing questionable deals into good deals would change.

The Roaring '80s

Aunt Mae was living in Arizona with her son, Howie, and daughter-in-law, Lana. Howie said they were struggling and bankrupt. He could not find work. I invited him to come to New York and live with me. I had plenty of room in my condo and spent most of my time at work. He managed to find a job as a truck driver and was able to send money home.

Tess was still living in Florida with Lester. She had her last child, Michael when she was forty-seven years old. Alexis, Doreen, and Robert were grown by the time Michael arrived. Uncle Abe and Jean were still living in Co-Op City in the Bronx. Sadly, Jean had Alzheimer's disease, but Abe, ever the caretaker, was there to watch over her.

My father and Natalie were still living in Chattanooga, Tennessee. I often thought that time and my success would bring some degree of healing to our relationship, but I was never entirely comfortable around them. They visited me occasionally and stayed in the condo, and I was always on pins and needles throughout their stay.

After Mark sold his Butcher Shop in Forest Hills, he went to work for his old boss, Ludwig, who owned a huge meat market in the Brighton Beach area of Brooklyn. Soon after, Ludwig offered him a partnership in the business because he was getting on in years, and he knew Mark fit the bill.

Mark moved into a studio apartment with his dog only one block from the store. One day when he was walking the dog, he saw an attractive young woman about to enter an apartment. His dog jumped on her, and soon he found out her name was Mira Zerdanovski, a newly arrived immigrant from Israel.

They became fast friends and he invited her to accompany him to Steve and Angela's New Years Party to welcome in

1985. Needless to say, we were all very impressed. Soon Mira moved in with Mark.

The year 1986 was a memorable one for my family. On June 23, 1986, Stephen's wife, Angela, gave birth to my first grandchild, Alexandra. Where had the years gone? It seemed like yesterday I was a young mother with three children of my own.

Of course, every birth made me think of my Donald. I still missed him as much as they day he died. Nat showed up for family events and special occasions, but neither of us had much to say to each other. Our marriage and our early years together had become a faded memory.

Eventually Mark and Mira purchased a bungalow in Sheepshead Bay area close to the store. At that point they decided to get married. On July 15, 1986, a local Rabbi came to perform the small wedding ceremony at their new home. According to Jewish tradition, a quorum of ten Jewish men (a *minyan*) is required to be present.

My partner, Josh, had become a part of our family, and he was part of the *minyan* for Mark's wedding. In many ways, I think I felt like Josh was my third son, not that anyone could every replace my Donald.

Josh

Josh had an active social life in the gay community. He was known for being promiscuous. One night he picked up a young man in Forest Park, and he decided to bring him home. This was not unusual behavior for Josh, but as it turned out, this guy was just sixteen years old. He was a savvy street kid who saw an opportunity to make a buck.

There were many times I had pulled Josh out of tight situations with different lovers. This fellow was a challenge! He sent me a letter saying he was just sixteen, and he hinted that he was going to inform the authorities that Josh had been sleeping with a minor.

I was livid! This was a blackmail set up. Aunt Mae's son, Howie, was living with me at the time. Howie, Josh and I hatched a plan. I decided to call the kid's bluff and tell him that I owned everything. I told him his blackmail attempt would not milk a penny out of me, and I wouldn't hesitate to call the cops and report him for prostitution and attempted black-mail. I had to get this guy out of our lives. Little did he know he had met his match!

I was getting tired of rescuing Josh. I loved the fast pace of our business, the wheeling and dealing and living on the dangerous side, but I had to be serious. This was my last hur-rah, and I had to make the business successful. I was the con-servative one of our team when it came to spending. Josh was just the opposite. He insisted that we renovate saying I was behind the times. We added cubicles and a state-of-the-art phone system that cost a small fortune.

Even though we had already been there for two years, we decided to have a re-grand opening to bring in business and re-coop our expenses. We ran multiple ads, hung flyers and contacted every media source. The big day arrived, and along with it, a massive storm. Our brand new phone system went down, and our hopes of making any money, went down with it. We could hear the phones ringing but had no way to answer. With every ring, we felt like a potential sale was lost. The phone rang most of the day, and I was so frustrated I cried. We had spent thousands only to watch it slip through our fingers. We had no choice but to replace the entire phone system and insurance did not cover "natural disasters".

The business was growing, but Josh still insisted on spending every penny of profit. Josh always wanted bigger and better. Our Christmas parties that we could ill afford had become the talk of the entire neighborhood of Century 21s and the local real estate companies. We spent thousands on "show" because we wanted to create a positive social image.

The draw that each of us received had grown but was still not enough to cover our living expenses. I began to gamble that the "next big deal" would not only get us out of debt but also make us big money. I'm not sure whether it was a gamble or my only hoping that after so much time and money the big payoff was just around the corner.

Josh thought the answer was to look influential, so he insisted on leasing the second floor of the building we rented. He thought if we, as the principle partners, had our offices upstairs in a well-decorated suite, surely we would get bigger sales opportunities. This move doubled our rent and put us deeper in debt, but I went along with it, still gambling and hoping for the best. I had heard, "You are out of date and old fashioned" so many times I think I began to believe it against sound reason. I trusted Josh on one hand but felt like I was living on "lady luck" on the other.

We moved into spacious offices upstairs, each of us on opposite ends of the large room. The first thing, Josh insisted that we redecorate. Of course, he did have a degree from Fashion Institute of Technology as an interior designer and loved to look good. I knew our budget could not accommodate redecorating. We were paying the overhead for forty agents and our phone bill alone was often three thousand dollars or more a month.

A New Dynamic

In spite of our huge monthly expenses, we were growing and we received many awards. We went to Century 21 events in Las Vegas. Josh's parents lived in California, and we all became so close, I considered them family. Josh even visited my father and Natalie in Chattanooga on occasion.

About five years into our business, Josh met a Columbian named Jose. He called himself Omar. They became inseparable. It was obvious that Josh was in a serious relationship. It clicked just how serious this relationship was when Josh gave away his beloved cat, Menachem, at Omar's request. I never thought I would see the day he would leave his cat.

Josh and I had always been very close, but now that Omar was in the picture, things began to change. Omar was an assistant chef at a restaurant in the World Trade Center. Not long after Omar moved in with Josh, he said he wanted to bring Omar on board to train as an agent. I said, "Josh, you know the old adage; you don't shit where you eat."

Before Omar was in the picture, I had brought in Mira, Mark's wife to train as an agent. Josh insisted that she should not be there, and I was accused of playing favorites. It broke my heart when I told her that she should not come upstairs too often because the other agents were complaining. I started a relationship with my new daughter-in-law on the wrong foot! This would have a lasting long term effect on my family bond with Mark and Mira. Now that Josh wanted Omar as an agent, he had no problem turning his cheek to the rule of playing favorites.

Omar moved into the penthouse of the building in Kew Gardens with Josh. I was still living on the twelfth floor. Omar finally got his Gold Jacket. As a Spanish speaker, he met with many of our Spanish-speaking clients. This should have been a positive move and brought in more cash flow, but something was off. Six months passed and Omar had showed countless apartments available for rent, but the business never saw a dime of commission.

This was the first time I became suspicious of Josh's integrity. I had a sick feeling in the pit of my stomach that something was up. By this time, all of our business charge cards were maxed out. Josh's personal credit cards could no longer support the company or his lifestyle. My credit cards had also reached their limit, and we were using our personal credit lines to survive. I think I had been in denial, but Josh's assurances were hollow words on the bottom line. The situation with Omar and lack of commissions bothered me enough that I knew I had to have a heart to heart talk with Josh.

We talked, but I felt no reassurance. Josh repeated the same old lines, and I had no reply. He thought I was jealous and behaving unfairly about Omar. Our conversations were no longer filled with excitement for the future or the thrill of building our business. The close relationship we had had for years was gone. I felt ignored, as though we were not actually communicating. Omar had not only taken my place as his confidant, but Josh had also shared the most intimate details of our business with him. I was a fifty-fifty partner, but somehow Omar now acted as though the blood, sweat and tears it took to build this business was his doing.

We were living from hand-to-mouth and all of our living expenses were coming out of the business. Those were the days of endless credit cards, with banks issuing an unending line of credit. The more credit cards we had, the more we spent. Every time we had a good deal and an influx of cash, Josh decided we should spend the money to grow or update something. I argued, yelled and screamed, but he always had his way.

Every argument was met with comments like, "You are too old and behind the times," or "This is how business is done today." I was in too deep, in my mid-fifties and afraid to lose everything. Josh applied for a business loan with a local bank to carry us over. I felt like I had no choice so I just went along. I was pouring every ounce of energy and every moment of time to make a success of what I thought would be my last career. I often thought of my family and wished I had the time to spend with them.

The spending continued. Even though we had more than forty agents in our office, in real estate the deal only counts when the property closes. Potential commissions could take months! It took a lot of energy and money to support the massive overhead. We were on the road to bankruptcy. If we hit that wall, there would be no way we could borrow money. We blew through the business loan like dry fall leaves on a windy day. Soon, we found ourselves short of cash and Josh said it was my turn to take out a loan. I felt like I had no choice if we were going to survive.

Josh filled out the loan application to the same bank using the same collateral as he had on his loan the year before. The loan officer thought it looked very similar to Josh's loan application and connected the dots, recognizing we were both connected to the same firm using the same collateral. Our loan was denied and our account was flagged to alert the proper authorities for any irregularities.

We were scared shitless! Without continuing cash flow, our resources were gone. Reality smacked us between the eyes. There was nowhere to run, nowhere to hide and no more denial. That sick feeling in the pit of my stomach was not in my head and settled in my heart. We were very lucky that the bank manager, who we had known since we went into business together, convinced the loan officer not to report us. We felt like he saved our lives.

An attorney who was a friend of Josh's suggested that he file for personal bankruptcy. Omar was still living and working with Josh. They were together all of the time, at work, in social situations and at home. It had been a slow process, but as Josh and Omar grew closer, Josh and I grew farther apart. I was feeling like an outsider with my own business partner. Instead of Omar and Josh welcoming me as a family member, I had lost a family member. I finally accepted that I had been replaced.

I had no choice but to confront Josh and get to the heart of so many issues that it felt like a tsunami bearing down on us. Our last conversation was like nothing I had ever experienced with Josh! He became so defensive. The years of trust and friendship dissolved as he slipped over the line of decency and became outright nasty. He called me foul names, assaulted me with curse words and blame, and he even threatened me with physical harm.

Break-ins and Breakdowns

I was in shock! I had never been spoken to like this by anyone in my life, much less someone I regarded as a trusted partner and family member. We had our disagreements and even arguments over the years, but Josh had never been nasty and threatening. I felt like a close family member had just stabbed me in the heart. I barely held it together as I left the office feeling bewildered and defeated.

I called Mark sobbing as I tried to explain what happened. Mark had never seen me like this. I had no idea Mark would respond as he did. I went back upstairs trying to make sense of what had just happened between Josh and me.

A short time later, to my total surprise, Mark walked into our office carrying an iron rod in his hand. He didn't even glance my way. He stormed over to Josh, who was cowering in fear. Mark walked aggressively towards Josh, his face contorted in anger. He grabbed the scruff of Josh's collar and shoved him in the corner.

Josh began to tremble as a wet stain spread across his pants and a look of sheer panic covered his face. Even though Mark never laid a finger on him, Josh's fear was evident. I was still searching my mind for what could have happened to make Josh behave that way and trying to understand why Mark was there.

I heard Mark say, "Are you going to treat my mother with respect?" His voice was calm, but it was clear that there was only one answer he expected.

Still cowering in the corner, Josh was pale and leaning over to vomit as he nodded yes.

I stayed home the next two days. It finally occurred to me that maybe Josh was trying to force me out of our business.

After all we had been through together, I couldn't believe that this could be a possibility. As I looked at reality, I realized that he and Omar were creating a new plan, especially since we had not seen any of Omar's commissions go into the business. My denial of what I had been sensing for a long time hit me like a hurricane. The truth was hard to bear.

I managed to pull myself together and headed back to work only to find that I had been locked out! The locks on the doors to our upstairs office had been changed! I discovered that Josh had gone to the police right after Mark had scared the shit out of him. He told the cops that a neurotic employee that he intended to fire would show up to cause trouble. He asked them to be on the lookout and said he might need their protection.

I was furious! This was half my office, half my business, and all of my heart and soul. We had built the business together, and he had no right to treat me that way! My anger got the best of me. I got a hammer and smashed the lock on the door determined to go into my office.

Our staff was downstairs and, for the most part, other than Omar, I am sure they had no idea what was going on, or that either of us had filed for bankruptcy.

Josh was inside. He called the police telling them the employee he had warned them about was going crazy and had become violent. In minutes, two squad cars and four officers arrived. By their very approach, I knew they thought I was the violent intruder breaking in. They demanded that I step away from the doors and get out of the building.

I was desperately trying to tell them I was not an employee that could be fired. I owned half of the business! The officers made me stand outside the building, oblivious to my words. The female cop had no compassion. In fact, she was downright cruel to me and refused to hear my explanation. They believed that I was the crazed woman they had been warned about. By this time, our employee's downstairs were watching the drama unfold, confused as to what could possibly be going on.

I had made a prior appointment with a bankruptcy attorney, so I had corporate papers with me that explicitly stated I owned half of the company. I was shoving the papers at the officers franticly saying, "This is my business. Please listen to me!" My heart was racing. How did this happen?

I had spent many years being very involved in social and community events and through these activities I developed numerous contacts. I collected myself as best I could and said, "Rose Rothchild, the secretary of the Corona Community Board, is a good friend of mine. Please let me call her."

One of the officers recognized her name and accompanied me as I stepped into a small shop next door. I got Rose on the phone. After trying my best to explain the circumstances, I handed the phone to the officer, and he heard the facts. Rose convinced him to allow me to give him my papers showing me as an owner, which he shared with the other officers. While he was with them sorting out the truth, I steadied myself and called my lawyer.

Now that the facts were straight, the officers walked me into the building, and they asked Josh to step outside. I called Mark and Stephen, telling them what had happened and that I intended to stay at work. The officers said we each needed to work in a separate area. I would work downstairs and Josh would stay upstairs.

How did my life come to this? A dark depression took root in my bones. I had never been one to give up or feel sorry for myself, but I was nearing sixty years old and this situation was taking its toll. The loss of a dream I had worked so hard for, and the loss of the physical comforts of home and transportation were overwhelming.

The time and investment I had made building my future disappeared in the blink of an eye, or so it seemed. The reality that this situation had been unfolding for some time and that maybe I had been in denial or not savvy enough to see it coming was hard to face. My feelings welled up to interrupt every waking thought as I struggled to make sense of the enormity of this change in circumstance. Most of all, hitting me in the deepest recesses of my being, was the realization that I had been betrayed by someone I considered a trusted member of my family.

A New Reality

My whole reality changed and my personality changed along with it. I became paranoid as well as depressed. Josh had now become an enemy. He had his friends call me, making threats by telling me that Mark was going to go to jail. Josh rallied his friends in the gay community, and I felt like a hate campaign was being waged against me. It was all I could bear to realize the dream of my real estate business was on the verge of collapse, and I had an unknown future ahead of me. The psychological torment from someone who had been a trusted partner and family member sent me into a state of utter despair.

I had been a boss at the agency which did not always allow for close relationships with sales agents. For years, I had spent very little time having a social life, devoting myself to the business. What little time remained during the week, I spent with my family.

I had two good friends who were agents that understood my pain. They were Peter Bronson and Steve Brown. They brought me food and were a spot of kindness in some very dark hours. I was in a daze. This was the darkest state of being I had ever experienced. Maybe I survived my childhood because of the innocence and resilience of youth. Donald's death was horrific, but I had a young family that needed me, and I had to rise up for them. For the first time in my life, standing on the balcony of my Kew Gardens condominium with my hopes shattered, I considered suicide.

Mark was so afraid for my safety that he insisted on hiring an enormous black bodyguard who was an ex-prize fighter to sit with me while I was at the office. Josh went to the police to complain the bodyguard was unnecessary and that he was scaring away clients. The police asked me to come to the station and explain my reasons for feeling like I needed this kind of protection. As if life wasn't stressful enough, now I was being grilled by the police! I told them about the threats and that I feared for my safety. The chief of police decided to assign a detective, who would also serve as a bodyguard, to stay with me while I was at the office.

I went to see Bob Cassandra and laid the cards on the table. Up to this point, he had no idea what drama had been unfolding at his property. Nearly a month had passed since Josh had locked me out. During this time I had filed for bankruptcy, my car had been repossessed and I was taking the bus, often in below zero weather. Angela bought me a long down coat, to make the ride tolerable. My condo had been foreclosed, and I was given a date to vacate the premises. I was out of money and out of the will to fight. I filled Bob in on the situation. At this point, we owed him sixty thousand dollars. He went to meet with Josh. Of course, he was looking after his own interest.

Bob offered Josh a chance to pay him back and he asked Josh to give me ten thousand dollars and dissolve our relationship. My lawyer said if I took the ten grand that I would not be eligible for bankruptcy protection, and I would be liable for nearly a quarter of a million dollars I owed to creditors.

I was at the end of my will to continue. I had no more fight in me. Josh accepted Bob Cassandra's offer. I was out. I heard through Peter Bronson that Josh's brother, who was a successful real-estate agent in California, had come to his aid. Stephen and Angela asked me to move in with them. I was penniless, helpless and deeply depressed. I accepted their offer as I was approaching my sixtieth birthday.

Life with Stephen and Angela

Stephen and Angela lived in West Babylon, a neighborhood of Long Island, New York. My sons rented a U-Haul and moved everything I owned into the basement of Stephen's home. I had always accepted whatever came my way, but this situation? I felt like there was no way out, much less up. I had always taken great pride in my looks. My hair was always done, and I loved dressing the part for whatever situation came my way. I had fallen apart. I was so depressed I didn't care what I wore; my body was falling apart and my hair grew into a knotted mass of gray tangled curls. I was in desperate need of dental care with no means to afford it. Mark and Mira were very kind and gave me an allowance of forty dollars a week. Mira would take me to get my hair cut. It was the smallest of kindnesses that meant so much.

I did all I could to be a productive part of their household. My grandchildren, Alexandra and Elizabeth, were six and four-and-a-half years old. I took them to school and helped with their care so Angela was free to finish her nursing degree. When I had a few dollars, I would take the girls for ice cream.

I overheard my daughters-in-law, Angela and Mira, discussing what a burden I was to the family. I was seldom included in their family events. I was living with family, but feeling more alone and isolated than I had ever been. Angela's Italian mother would often say to her, "I kept my mother-in-law for forty years! Don't do it, Angela!"

The psychological effect this isolation had on me was devastating. I was so emotionally drained it took a toll on my health. My legs were constantly getting knots of unbearable cramps, and I took so many aspirins it caused me to become anemic. I contracted a massive gum disease, which I now know can also affect your heart. I was completely falling apart!

No matter what my life circumstance had been, I had always maintained my self-esteem. For the first time, I hated myself. As my misery grew, Angela became more unwelcoming. Her mother, instead of having an ounce of compassion, was always filling her head with the idea that I was sponging off of them. I often holed up in the basement paralyzed with shame, fear, and despair. Everyone around me was sure I was broken, and I began to believe it.

My gums got so bad that I needed medical attention. Angela contacted my father, and he was kind enough to send money to help. Now in his mid-eighties, I was glad he responded, but we were far from having a close father-daughter relationship.

Still A Broker

I was still a real estate broker and took a job with Prudential Real Estate in the village of Babylon. I knew New York City like the back of my hand. The community of Babylon was a whole new area to become familiar with. Thankfully, Stephen loaned me his station wagon. It required a lot of driving to learn a new territory. Of course, there were no cell phones or global positioning devices in those days. We made our way with paper maps and beepers. I spent a lot of time driving around because I understood that no sales meant no commissions.

I hated being a burden to my children because I was penniless. I had hit the bottom of the barrel and I felt like shit. I felt like I was as despised as a leper, a dope addict or an alcoholic. I was neither. Mark gave me forty dollars a week to cover my expenses at Prudential Real Estate. Of course, I had to call him to ask him for the money or meet him at work. I flashed back to being a little girl taking the subway to Harlem to get a lousy quarter from my father, which only deepened my shame and feeling of self-hatred.

Fortunately, I had stayed in touch with old friends. As difficult as the situation was, I had other sources of support, although I didn't have the money to go out, much less the energy. I had also kept my contact list from the days in real-estate. While I was living with Stephen and Angela, I had heard that Lennie Bongers was divorced. I thought his home might be for sale so I gave him a call. A woman named Barbara Howe answered the phone and said that Lennie was living with his parents, Madeline, and Otto, in Atlanta. It seems that Lennie had given that phone number to several ladies, and Barbara figured I was just one of the girls he kept on a string. Barbara and I had a great conversation, and we laughed when she realized I had rented the upstairs space from his parents after Nat and I separated. In fact, she invited me to visit her in Lindenhurst.

Barbara and I had a lot in common. She was a widow, intelligent and fun to talk to. She had a very successful career working for the government sector of Nassau-Long Island. Our friendship grew from that moment of happenstance, and we became very close friends. She helped make my life tolerable while I was living with the children. When the situation was unbearable at Stephen's, which was often, I spent the night in her guest room. Eventually, she moved to Atlanta to be with Lennie. Our friendship never ended, and as I write this, we still speak to each other often on the phone.

Finally, I had a potential sale that could net a five thousand dollar commission. The home was across the street from where Angela's sister and brother-in-law lived. I saw no problem that they were a mixed race couple, a black woman, and a white man. All of a sudden, grumbling arose from the neighborhood like a swarm of hornets. Angela's father called me a dummy in his broken English. The couple got wind of the racism and hatred and became afraid of vigilantes. In the hit and miss world of real estate, I was finally ready to make a sale, and the bottom fell out. Stephen said, "Today the blacks; tomorrow the Jews."

Mark had been angry with me from the time I left Nat in 1973 until 2006. He never missed a moment to give me a dig or bring me to tears. In so many ways, his verbal abuse and hostility toward me was much like his father. That was the primary reason I had left Nat. In the same way I could not reason with Nat or change his behavior toward me, history was repeating itself through Mark, and I felt just as helpless. No matter what happened between us, at some deep level, through the pain and hostility, we never stopped loving each other. Mark was always there for me in the worst of situations and helped me countless times. No doubt our relationship had an effect on his wife, Mira. I was always proud of how hard Mark worked. His long-time partnership with Ludwig in the butcher business paid off. Eventually, Mark and Mira bought a beautiful home in Harbor Isle, a private island surrounded by the Atlantic Ocean, just off Long Beach, New York.

Pink Convertible, Fur Coats, and Diamonds

A referral from a Prudential Real Estate office in Babylon came my way. A Jewish family wanted to locate to Long Island within walking distance of a synagogue. This was right up my alley. I started to research the areas they were interested in and noticed my gas tank was empty. I barely had enough gas to make it home. I was so desperate for money I robbed my grandchildren's piggy bank. I had stooped to an all-time low. However, this led to an unexpected opportunity.

The president of a Jewish Synagogue in Lindenhurst, Long Island, invited me to Friday services. Unlike me, I went and I was warmly welcomed. It felt wonderful to be treated like a person, no one having any idea of the suffering and struggles I was going through. I was invited to a special event they were having the following week. I needed to get out so I accepted. Little did I know the president of the synagogue had something specific in mind.

I was invited to sit at a table where I was introduced to the president's father-in-law. He was an older gentleman in his late eighties wearing a horrible black toupée that reminded me of the one Georgie Jessel used to wear. Multiple diamond rings with huge rocks decorated his bent arthritic fingers. He wore an even bigger diamond in his tie. It was almost comical, but he seemed like a nice old man.

The old gentleman invited me to a movie, and for some reason, I was unable to refuse. He offered to pick me up at five in the evening that coming Wednesday. I was embarrassed that my family, or anyone else I knew, might see me with this old man, so I agreed to meet him at one of many buildings their family owned. As I was waiting outside second guessing my decision, my thoughts were interrupted by the obnoxious bellowing honk of a car horn that sounded more like the death throes of a sick cow. An antique pink convertible Rolls Royce, custom built from a kit, rolled alongside the building to pick me up. "Oh my god!", I thought to myself, "I am so glad he didn't pick me up at the kids' house."

We went to the movies, and I was grateful it was dark. Afterward, we went to a Chinese restaurant where everyone seemed to know him. He asked for the chef to come to our table, thanked him for the excellent dinner, and gave him a twenty dollar tip, making a grand gesture out of it. He asked me if I would like to see his home. Curiosity got the best of me and I said yes. After all, he was a little old man in his eighties, and I hadn't had this much diversion from my worries in quite a while.

The outside of his home was modest, but as soon as he opened the door I was assailed with the gaudiest, most outrageous decorations from furniture to art and window treatments that I had ever seen. Selling real estate, I had seen a lot! He proudly gave me the grand tour. His closet was the same size as his bedroom and was filled with expensive suits, jackets, and shoes. Then, puffed up with pride, he showed me the ladies closet. It was overflowing with fur coats, capes, dresses, jackets, shoes and handbags.

I was still reeling from how gaudy the place was and at all these women's clothing when he offered me a cup of tea. I was grateful to head downstairs and have a seat. He told me that the furs belonged to his long-deceased wife. Many of the other clothes belonged to a woman he had been living with for years who had just moved to Florida to live with her children. As I was trying to wrap my brain around it all, he popped the question. He asked me if would I move in with him and take her place. He said he would support me if I would be his live-in companion. The whole ridiculous evening, from the pink Rolls-Royce with an obnoxious horn to the tipping of the chef and showing off the furs began to make sense. In my most diplomatic manner, I refused his offer.

Hope Rises

One Sunday morning I woke up, and I don't know how or why, but a change had come over me. For the first time in almost nine months, the darkness had lifted from my soul. I was filled with hope. It was as though God had seen my plight, and I was given a reprieve.

I remembered that summer I spent at the Webertuck Kosher Hotel so many years ago as a young woman. I remembered hearing the "old ladies" (who were probably the age I was currently) lamenting, "I could have;" "I should have," and "I would have." I remembered making the decision that I was never going to live my life with regret. I was not going to be an old woman who sat around and complained about the life I had missed. I was going to live!

I got out of bed with a new determination that day. Enough was enough! I was resilient and would rise up in spite of my circumstances. This situation would not define the rest of my life. I felt as though the weight of the world had lifted off my shoulders. I can only believe that God, in a supernatural way, intervened on my behalf. Despite my outward physical condition, as soon as my spirit began to mend, my body followed.

I picked up the employment section of the *New York Times* and saw that Macy's was having a career seminar. I looked in the mirror and finally saw myself looking back. I fixed my hair, put on make-up and my best clothes. Thoughts bounced through my mind with hope. If I could sell space to mall tenants and real estate, surely I could be successful as a Macy's salesperson.

Macy's hired me on the spot, and I was assigned to the handbag department of their store in the Huntington Mall in Long Island. It was a draw against commission position. The area was enormous. There were bags of every size, shape and color. I felt that old determination rise up, and I decided I would learn the ropes and be the best at my job. I was back! I kept my job at Prudential Real Estate working part-time, but Macy's would provide a steady income.

Most of the staff in that department was twenty-something. Their primary objective seemed to be to gather together and chat. Life in the handbag department offered them a personal social hour to re-hash the events of the weekend or the drama of the night before. We had little in common except for our physical location. I set out to conquer my territory. I saw every customer as a potential sale and commissions were rolling in.

Just weeks into my newfound success, I was surprised to be called in by my manager and assigned to the stock room. It was backbreaking work of hauling and opening boxes and climbing up and down a tall ladder for most of the day. It seems the other girls had complained about me. They thought I was too aggressive and taking all their customers. They had no idea how motivated I was and what this opportunity meant to me.

I was taken aback but desperately needed the job, so I did my best in the stock room, coming home physically exhausted at night with no commissions. I thrived on attention and interaction with people, so it was a double blow. About a month after I was assigned to the stock room, I was called into the office by my manager. She told me that since I had been working on the sales floor, department sales were up more than forty percent. She apologized and asked me if I would go back on the floor as a sales person. What a relief and affirmation!

Shortly after I was back in sales, the store policy changed. There would be no more commissions except in the shoe department. Commissions were the lifeline that would allow my independence. I immediately requested and was granted, a transfer to the shoe department. My reputation as a go-getter preceded me. I had learned from my experience and worked hard to cultivate positive relationships with my fellow employees so I would not appear to be a threat. I learned the ropes and was getting along well with my peers and feeling secure in my job.

During this time, I noticed a sign in the break room at Macy's that offered free psychological services for employees. I had greatly benefited from visits in the past and decided to take advantage of the service. It was time for the next step in my independence.

I was ready to move out of Stephen and Angela's basement and find my own place. Just as that thought welled up, I was listening to the radio on my way to work and heard about a "home share" program in the village of Babylon. The idea was for widows or widowers who had extra space in their homes and needed extra income or companionship to share their home for a small fee. I had been to about half-a-dozen homes when I was sent to a home in Deer Park, owned by a widow named Charlotte Silver. Her husband had died almost a year earlier, and we were both willing to take a chance on one another. My rent would be three-hundred and seventy-five dollars.

I had not told Stephen and Angela about the home share program. Ironically, that same week Stephen said he and Angela would like to speak to me on Sunday morning. I felt like I had become a burden to them, and I knew in my heart that they were going to ask me to pay rent or to move out.

I said, "Let me speak first." I told them about my plans and they said nothing. I had saved a small amount of money from my job at Macy's and was able to afford all the expenses it took to move. Mark and Stephen, once again, got a U-Haul and packed all of my belongings and moved me into Charlotte's house.

Charlotte Silver was delightful, funny, and intelligent. She was in her late sixties, young to be widowed. Because we were close in age, we had a lot in common. She was also Jewish, and we celebrated the traditional holidays together. Her ample figure was a testament to her love of eating. We often referred to ourselves as the "golden girls", after a favorite television show at that time.

Charlotte introduced me to her circle of friends, and I was feeling more like myself as time passed. Her son lived nearby and she invited him and his family for dinner often. I asked Stephen and Angela and my grandchildren. Charlotte and I chipped in on meals and special occasions, and as I continued to enjoy her company, life became more normal every day. I was regaining my sense of self-worth and was happy for opportunities to socialize. There was still little communication with Mark and Mira so I seldom saw them.

Chattanooga, Tennessee

I continued to work at Macy's and was doing very well. I was burned out by real-estate and resigned from Prudential. I reconnected with old friends and a sense of normalcy returned to my life. I reconnected with Natalie and my father, now in their mid-eighties and still living in Chattanooga, Tennessee. We talked three or four times a week, something we had never done before. Natalie began to confide in me. She told me my father was becoming very forgetful and that he was often nasty and just downright mean to her. I also shared some of my struggles, and I was open about my vulnerabilities.

Eventually, Natalie called and said, "Your father and I would like you to come and live with us. We can help each other." She said they would give me the house when they passed on and about four thousand dollars a year in stocks. After all these years of a hot and cold relationship, I felt like they were extending an olive branch.

At this point, I was feeling like a step-grandmother. I knew I could not live with Charlotte forever and saw this as an opportunity to build a future for myself. I talked things over with the psychiatrist who I was still seeing, and she encouraged me to make the move. Natalie never had children and I was my father's only child. I also wanted to be a good daughter. My relationship with my own children wasn't working, and I thought I could step up and do the right thing. I mulled things over for about six months and thought this was the only way to build a future for myself and that, at long last, I might have a positive father-daughter relationship.

I decided I had nothing to lose. I was moving to Chattanooga, Tennessee. The Deep South. As I was wrapping things up in New York, I found out I was eligible for unemployment, an unexpected boon. I was six months shy of my sixty-second birthday and decided to take early social security. I was told that if my former husband should precede me in death, and I was sixty-five or older, I might also be eligible for a portion of his social security. I felt better knowing I had some small means of support for my future life in Tennessee.

I had my clothes shipped via U.P.S. and left my furniture behind. I bought a one-way ticket on a Greyhound bus for fifty-nine dollars. In my conversations with Natalie, I understood the expectation was for me to help drive them places, help with shopping, cooking, and cleaning. They were sleeping in separate bedrooms but began sharing a room so I could use the second bedroom.

From City to Country

I arrived in Chattanooga and received a warm welcome. I settled in, hopeful and open to the possibilities of the future. My father had not aged well. He was bent over and his twisted body was a match for his negative personality. It seemed any good I remembered had diminished and his pessimistic qualities about life had magnified. He was very nasty to Natalie and called her disgusting names. It was clear his dementia had taken root and was growing worse by the day. My father had always been a mean human being, but in the end, life boiled down to its essence, he was toxic to be near. If their small dog didn't take care of business fast enough, his foot would fly out with a blow to its side.

Natalie, who was never very attractive, looked much better as an older woman. She was a native Chattanoogan and still socialized with many of her childhood friends and was very active in the synagogue. A group of her friends had weekly gatherings for card games and social time at each others homes. I was relieved when she left the house, even for a short while. When the women came to her house, I could not help but notice how slow she had become, even when it came to deciding what card to play. Eventually, the group asked her to bow out when it became evident she couldn't keep up. Every morning I heard Natalie screaming from some nightmare or unimaginable pain. She never talked about it, and I was hesitant to ask, but it was very unnerving.

Natalie had a nephew, Harold, who was the apple of her eye. Harold was married and had six children. He was also blind in one eye, which Natalie blamed on her sister-in-law, saying if she had paid closer attention to him when he was a child, this accident never would have happened. That was Natalie. She always blamed someone for everything she perceived she could have done better. Her scorn was even turned on Harold's wife, Rose.

Just after I moved in, I noticed Harold was a frequent visitor. His resentment of me was clear, although I'm not sure why he took such a dislike to me. Later, I came to believe because of the many years he had served as their handyman, he resented the fact that I was offered my father's home and a share of stock when they died. He was well aware of their financial situation, and no doubt, Natalie told him of the arrangement they had made with me.

I met a friend of Natalie's, Reba Bok, and we became good friends. She was very bright; she and Natalie both enjoyed the stock market. I had no investments at the time, but Reba and I had other things in common. As in so many other instances, Reba would come back into my life with wisdom when I needed it the most.

Chattanooga was quite an adjustment from New York. I was learning my way around and adjusting to a new city and an entirely new culture. I helped prepare their meals and decided I would do a significant amount of housekeeping every day to feel like I was pulling my weight. My father wanted to go to the mall every day for his social hour with his senior friends. It offered an indoor environment and a place to walk on even surfaces. It also gave him a wide open place to voice his disdain at humanity.

This was when I noticed how deeply racist he was. If a mixed race couple walked by he would point and sneer with his face contorted in hate. He would say loud enough for everyone to hear "Look at that, will you just look at that!"

I was not easily ashamed or embarrassed, but I was utterly humiliated by his hatred. Had he forgotten that he was Jewish and the reason his parents moved to this country? I began to wonder what I had gotten into.

Some Things Never Change

I had been in Chattanooga less than a month when Natalie started to complain about my cooking and demanded I do things exactly as she wanted them. I was willing to try. Shortly afterward, she began to complain because I took daily showers, saying every other day would be enough. I offered to pay her ten dollars a month for the extra water.

It was becoming clear to me, the situation was not mutually beneficial. I was not just a helper or even a maid; I was their servant expected to obey every demand. There are many sayings about personal character. I should have realized something as defining as your character never changes.

Fortunately, Natalie had introduced me to a divorced woman named Sylvia who lived up the block. We had a lot in common and became close friends. Sylvia drove me around and showed me the city. We enjoyed spending time together and often had lunch together.

One Sunday afternoon, Sylvia dropped me back at home and Natalie shrieked at me, "Do you think I'm running a motel here?" She had no respect for me or any desire to help me regain my independence. It was clear she wanted to control my every move and expected me to be at her beck and call. Everything I had dreaded about her during my lifetime came flooding back to me. The way she had treated me as a young child had not changed. A zebra does not change its stripes.

Just as I was dealing with these feelings, my father sneered, "Look at those two, a couple of whores!"

Natalie's high pitched voice interjected, "I should never have introduced her to Sylvia."

I was furious. I snapped the television off, wheeled around and looked at my father and said, "How dare you! How dare you call your one and only daughter who is almost sixty-two a whore? Shame on you!"

He just stared at me with a blank look on his face. Natalie, for once, was entirely silent.

I retreated to my bedroom and closed the door. All I could think of was how the hell I was going to get out of there. Thank God for my unemployment and Social Security. I had managed to save three thousand eight hundred dollars. I had no idea where or how I was going to get out of that vile house, but there was no doubt I was going to get out, the sooner, the better.

Freedom!

The next morning I walked down to Sylvia's and burst into tears as I shared what had happened. She was in shock. I begged her to help me find an apartment. I decided I would use my small savings and find a used car. I had to have my freedom. Natalie, my father and I all remained civil to one another. All the while I was doing everything possible to quickly get out of their house.

I used every penny of my savings to buy a used car. It was old, but it would meet my needs and give me freedom. I stayed out of the house as long as I could every day. I went to the Hamilton Place Mall and interviewed for a position as a sales person. I knew my experience at Macy's was an asset. Belk's called the next day to offer me a job. I found a place in East-ridge called The Fountain Blue Apartments for two hundred and seventy-five dollars a month.

I was on a new high. I was motivated and could taste my freedom. A new future full of hope was unfolding. My head was spinning a mile a minute. In less than a week, I had a car, an apartment, and a new job. It was time to tell Natalie and my father that I was leaving. I let them know I would be gone the next day. Both of them were in a state of disbelief. They were counting on the fact that I was vulnerable and needed them for transportation, physical and financial support. I think it hit them hard that their "servant" would be gone.

The next morning I was up early, brimming over with excitement. I was packing all of my belongings in large black plastic trash bags. Natalie just stood and stared with her mouth hanging open.

As I put the final bag in my new car, Natalie came outside, and in her shrill voice she screamed like a fishwife at the top of her lungs. "God is going to punish you!"

I flashed back to the moment Mama Dora had said to Natalie, "Natalie, God is going to punish you for the vey you treat this child (speaking about me). You will never have a child of your own!" Natalie did have a miscarriage and never had children of her own. I believe Mama Dora's curse took root in Natalie's wicked heart.

I said, "God has already punished you!" She paled and had a strange look in her eyes. I believe at that moment Natalie also remembered exactly the curse Mama Dora spoke to her.

I drove away feeling free as a bird. My future was unknown, but I was excited, confident and determined. I settled into my new apartment and my new job at Belk's. I was determined to use all of my experience to be successful.

Belk's came with an unexpected benefit. I struck up a conversation with a woman who worked in the same department as I did. She was a top saleswoman, attractive and friendly. I admired her success. Kay Shore and I would become best friends. Eventually, she moved into the same apartment building, and we often visited each other. We had gone from a professional relationship to being like family. It was wonderful to have a close friend and confidant, especially as I adjusted to life in the South.

I hadn't spoken to Natalie or my father in more than a month. I decided to call and see how my father was doing. Natalie answered the phone and there was no comment, she just handed him the phone choosing to ignore me. Father asked me to come over, saying that he would meet me outside. He was well aware of the strained relationship between Natalie and me. Natalie stayed hidden behind the shutters as he got into my car and we went to see my new place.

All he could say was, "There is nothing I can do for you now. You understand she is my wife." I don't know if this was a lame apology, or his way of saying Natalie was in control of his life. The memory of being a child and having to take the subway all the way from the Bronx to 125th Street in Harlem came flooding back to me. As a child, I had traveled miles for a lousy quarter so I wouldn't interrupt my father's and Natalie's social life. I was a skinny young girl, short enough to slide under the subway turnstiles and save some money. I had to accept that some things would never change. Father's mental and physical health continued to decline as his dementia grew worse. I made the decision to visit him once a week regardless of how I was treated.

Harold's wife, Rose, invited me to a birthday party at their house. I needed to socialize, and even though Harold wasn't ideal company, at least it was an outlet. I got a call from Harold almost giddy as he told me not to show up for the party because Natalie had been invited. She was still mad at me and wouldn't come if I were there. As if that jab wasn't enough, he told me that I had been disowned and would no longer inherit my father's and Natalie's house or any stock. Harold's character was as hateful and as greedy as ever.

As rapidly as Father was declining, without me there to provide a taxi service, Natalie still allowed him to drive because she had given up driving years ago. They had an accident while he was driving, and they were lucky to come out of it alive. It aged his already fragile state of health. For a year following the accident I still picked him up once a week on Saturdays and Natalie still ignored me.

My father, born in Poland with the given name of Jankel Jakubavitz on October 10, 1907, died October 12, 1996, as an American named Jack Jamieson. My children came from New York with their families. Many people came from the local synagogue because Natalie was so involved in the Jewish community.

After the crowd had left and the children headed home, as Natalie and I sat *Shiva*, she said, "Let's let bygones be bygones." We maintained a civil relationship until Natalie died, in 1999.

Harold became the executor of Natalie's will. After her death, we went to see Natalie's lawyer together. As Father had alluded to before he died, and as Harold had so crassly told me, as my father's only child, I was left with nothing. Supposedly, I was left with stock worth $28,000, but it seems Natalie had sold the stock prior to her death, leaving me empty handed.

A friend suggested I see an attorney. Because Natalie knew so many people in the small city of Chattanooga, I had a hard time finding a lawyer. I found Flossie Weill In 1999. She was an excellent attorney, and through some very hard work, was able to resolve my issue, and I was given $28,000 worth of stock. Harold was so angry, what slim relationship we had disappeared.

Reba Bok, Natalie's old friend, suggested I find a financial advisor to help me invest. She recommended Michael Cartwright. He managed long-range investments for me that have been of great help. I am grateful for both Flossie and Michael and their expertise throughout the years. Michael has purchased at least five of my paintings.

Not Again!

I was getting older, and standing on my feet all day at Belk's was becoming more challenging as the days passed. I was almost sixty-five years old, and I realized I would need to find another way to support myself.

I had seen an abstract art exhibit at the Hunter Museum and thought that I could learn to paint as a means to earn a living. I used every free moment to take art lessons at the Hunter. The more I studied, the more I became sure that art was the key to my future. I learned to paint on silk, studied basic drawing and explored watercolor techniques and oil painting. I took one course after the other eager to learn all I could.

The single kindest thing my father ever said to me was, "I hope you'll paint a picture for me."

Natalie would say, "Oh, so now she thinks she's an artist!" I had learned never to expect any encouragement or affirmation from either of them.

I signed up for private lessons at Vickie Hardee's studio in Hixson. Tennessee, determined to learn the craft. When Stephen and Angela were able to visit, they always took paintings home, proud of my efforts and offering encouragement.

I had started at Belk's in 1994. In 1999, they sold out to Dillards. I received a fifty dollar a month pension for life after five years of service. While in wasn't much, I knew I would have art supplies for life. Dillards was going very well, and I continued to work in the shoe department.

The shoe department was the only area in the store with a draw against commission. That meant I was given a salary as an advance each pay period, which was considered a predetermined draw. I was expected to make my draw (and more) each pay period. The draw was deducted from my commission each pay period. It was a tough job because I had no control over customer volume or the offseason.

The manager loved me because I was a hard worker and go-getter. On the other hand, just like at Macy's, the other employees didn't like me because I was always on my toes and worked very hard for my commissions. They accused me of stealing their customers. They had no idea how hard I needed to work just to pay the bills and how much I counted on those commissions to make ends meet.

My friend, Lucianne, also worked in the shoe department. She was from Brazil and married to Ricardo, a fellow New Yorker. She warned me that other sales associates were out to get me, so I wasn't surprised. I never "stole" anyone's customers. The manager went on vacation, and I was fired by the acting manager. It was Macy's all over again! Lucianne and Ricardo eventually moved to Brazil. We are still in touch, and they are proud owners of two of my paintings.

I applied for unemployment, but my claim was denied. Dillards claimed that I had not made enough commissions to equal my draw. That was a situation that was always in flux. It always came back around when we had a good season, or the store had a sale to bring in customers to the shoe department, something out of my control. I was in the hole for $2,400 dollars at one point but brought that down to just $50.00 dollars. I appealed their decision and won. Once again, I was looking for work. This was stressful, but it also fueled my determination to work and study and become a successful artist.

I was out of work for a few months when I was hired by Proffits Department Store to work in their shoe department. They loved my New York chutzpah! I stayed there until, with an enormous sigh of relief, I retired at age seventy-three. What a long crazy working career I had experienced. Now it was time to focus on art.

Friends Lucianne and Ricardo, "Lucy and Rickey," now live in Brazil. We still stay in touch. It was Lucianne who told me that the other sales associates at Dillard's department store were trying to force me out because they resented my competitive nature in sales.

An Artist in the Making

I was fortunate that Chattanooga's Hunter Museum of American Art had a broad variety of art covering many styles and periods. It was inspirational for a budding artist. Art lessons were offered at the Hunter, so I signed up for silk painting, basic drawing, watercolor and oil painting. I immediately felt that oil painting was my niche. Vicki Hardee was teaching at the Hunter and also offered private classes in her art studio on Hixson Pike. After I had finished my classes at the museum, I continued to study oil painting with Vicki at her studio.

With Vicki's encouragement, I decided it was time to explore college courses, and I enrolled at Chattanooga State. I thought about pursuing a degree in art, but the burden that all the additional studies required to get a degree was beyond what I was able to manage at that point in my life. At age sixty-five, I was able to audit classes. I studied ceramics and sculpture and realized that oil painting was the direction to pursue.

My first college art teacher, John Helseth, taught me the basics. I studied cubism, organic art, and basic drawing. Even the tools were brand new to me. From learning about different paper weights and textures to pencils, brushes and paints, art intrigued me. I knew with enough study I could unleash my potential. There were several other people in their sixties also auditing the class and this gave me confidence. I was still working at Belk's, and I arranged my schedule to work nights and weekends, shifts most people were happy to trade, so that I could spend my mornings at school.

I was so enthralled with art that I studied art history and art appreciation. There were many young, talented students in my classes and students that received much more recognition than I did, but I didn't let that intimidate me. I loved oil painting. The luxuriant colors of ochre, cadmium red, and Prussian

blue and so many other lush hues were perfect for the buildings of New York City. The buildings, bridges and subways
called for layers of texture just like the years of life that they
had seen. I loved the tools, from palette knives to a variety of
brushes and wide range of canvases. I had found my medium.
I decided that I was going to learn to paint well enough to
subsidize my income.

I was fortunate to have Michael Holsomback as a teacher. His critiques were always positive, and I found his style of
teaching very encouraging. He had a way of allowing each student to express their own distinct art form. New York City
was what I knew the best, and he encouraged me to follow my
heart. The paints exploded onto the canvas in vibrant, rich
colors, and the tall buildings and bridges I had spent my life
around began to emerge as favorite subjects. Soon subways
and trains followed. I would dream of the city and wake up
excited about expressing my visions on canvas.

At Chattanooga State I entered the student exhibit. I
was thrilled when someone actually wanted to buy one of my
paintings! It was an abstract oil painting I had done with a
palette knife. I wasn't ready to sell it, but the offer to buy it was
just the affirmation I needed. I was on my way to a new career.

In 2002, I approached Southern Arts and Framing as an
act of desperation. It was a close-knit community and I needed to get my name out. I sold the owner on the idea of a one-
woman exhibit. I split the cost of an ad with her and paid for
the opening reception. This left me absolutely broke, but I was
all in. I hung flyers everywhere I could think of, including the
lunch room at Proffits. It was a good turnout, and once again I
was hopeful that I could build a career as an artist.

I had heard about In-Town, a co-op gallery featuring the
work of over thirty local artists, and thought I would check
it out. The woman on duty was Dana Shavin. I asked how I
could become a member of In-Town Gallery. She curtly
replied, "You have to pay your dues."

Being a New Yorker, I wasn't easily intimidated by her attitude. She suggested that first I join AVA, the Association for Visual Arts, on Frazier Avenue, organized to promote local arts and the art community at large. When I was more experienced, I might consider In-Town Gallery. I joined AVA. As an official member, I was invited to participate in an upcoming holiday exhibit.

I brought in a painting, a cityscape of New York that I had just finished. It had sold before the exhibit opened for one hundred and seventy-nine dollars. I was thrilled! I was asked to bring in another painting for the opening reception. I brought in a second New York cityscape that sold at the reception. The third time around I brought in a fruit abstract I had painted early in my lessons but had no luck selling it. I realized I needed to paint what I knew the best – My City.

Michael Holsomback suggested I join the Creative Arts Guild in Dalton, Georgia. They loved my paintings. When

New York - *The Way It Was*

they opened a co-op art gallery nearby, it was the first opportunity I had to sell my work where I had significant exposure to the public.

My painting of the *911 Disaster at the World Trade Center* was one of the first paintings I sold.

New York Stock Exchange

In 2003, I had a one-woman exhibit at the co-op gallery and sold a painting of the World Trade Center, which had just fallen. The images of utter chaos with people running down the streets panic stricken, surrounded by smoke and fire, must have touched my customer in a meaningful way. I sold the painting for five hundred dollars. My love of New York City and that tragedy was an emotionally trying time, and it was expressed in my work. I began to get established as an artist and received quite a bit of recognition. Eventually, the co-op gallery closed, but the Creative Arts Guild continued, and I entered yearly exhibits.

Vicki Hardee, soon to be Vicki White, opened Studio 2 on the South Side of Chattanooga at 27 West Main Street. I was invited to join the studio, which charged a monthly membership fee. Members were able to show their work and expected to spend time helping operate the gallery. Vicki was newly married, and her husband, Roger, had admired my painting of the New York Stock Exchange, which she bought as a gift for him. I was so surprised because my style was not her taste, and I was amused at the thought of my painting in her home.

New Years Eve on Times Square

Roots

Ten years had passed since I had moved into that one bedroom apartment in Eastridge. I was working at Profitts part-time, but painting had become my life's ambition and my small apartment had become my studio. I had painted myself out of the apartment. The sofa was in the middle of the living room because canvases stood stacked against every wall, and every inch of wall space was covered with my paintings.

I began to look for a larger apartment when I noticed a "rent to sell" ad at Signal View condominiums. The owner was willing to hold the mortgage. I went to look and found the door of the second story townhouse unlocked. The moment I opened the door, I knew this was the place for me. It was $28,000 dollars and $4,500 for the down payment. After all those years in real estate, I had found the deal of a lifetime! I finally owned my own home. I felt secure and safe. I had plenty of room to paint and an affordable place to retire. After a few years, I was elected to the board of directors and was able to bring years of experience in real estate to the association.

I worked in Studio 2 every Saturday for a few years. I dedicated space in my home for use as a studio and began to work in earnest. This was a time of inspiration, and I produced a significant amount of work during this period. I was extremely motivated, and my old knack for promotions served me well. I sold many of my paintings through the studio and worked very hard to promote the studio at large and had a solo exhibit at the studio.

Terri Zitrech Dennehy owned My Color Image, a Gallery on Frazier Avenue. It was a co-op gallery much like Studio 2. My work was there for almost two years, and I volunteered until she closed.

I was still taking lessons with Mike Holsomback after twelve years. During his class, I painted a portrait of a nude pregnant woman. I thought it was a beautiful expression of feminine beauty, and I looked forward to hanging it in Studio 2.

It seems a painting of a nude pregnant woman was far too liberal for Vicki and the other artists at the gallery. When it was my day to work, I would arrive to find the painting turned backward or hidden behind other paintings. Of course, I would immediately pull it out and put it on display. A female customer came in and fell in love with it. She returned and purchased the painting, which I once again had to dig out of a pile.

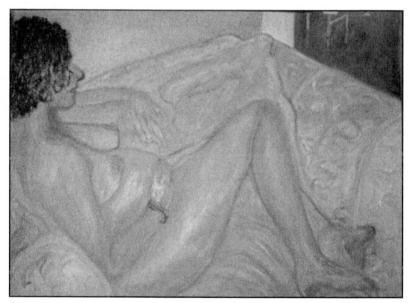

The painting I titled *A Baby* was purchased by a woman from Atlanta

Choosing Me

Becoming an accomplished artist was a process that took years. My first group showing was in 1998 and has continued. My first juried show was in 2002, and I have been a featured artist several times. I was slowly building a clientele and began to subsidize my income as I continued to take art classes. I relied on my salesmanship and promotion skills and began advertising for myself. I was invited to participate in many events throughout the city of Chattanooga, and I am grateful for the numerous articles I received in the *Times Free-Press* and many other local publications. Television and radio stations also covered my work.

I was honored to participate in the "Unmasked" fund raiser by creating a mask for the National Craniofacial Association, and I participated in many other fund raisers. Chattanooga

The mask at right is the creation of Roslynne Steinberg

Monday

Chattanooga Times Free Press
Monday, January 19, 2009
• • • +

NO CAUSE FOR PAUSE

By Holly Leber
HLEBER@TIMESFREEPRESS.COM

For some, reaching 70 years old might be a signal to slow down.
But for the Rev. Virgil Caldwell, 78, Roslynne Steinberg, 76, and Judge
Clarence Shattuck, 73, passing the septuagenarian mark is no cause for
a pause. Not, at least, in their pursuits of hobbies they love. A musician
and playwright, an artist and an athlete, these three Chattanoogans are
shaking off the shuffleboard stereotypes.

Judge
Clarence
Shattuck

Online:
See videos
of Virgil Caldwell,
Roslynne Stein-
berg and Clar-
ence Shattuck
talking about
their lifestyles

STILL DRIBBLING AT 73

Judge Clarence Shattuck spends his days on the bench in Hamilton County
General Sessions Court. He spends his evenings, on Tuesdays and Fridays at
least, on the basketball court.

"My first basketball hoop was a barrel hoop on the side of a slab barn," said
Judge Shattuck.

He grew up in Soddy-Daisy, playing baseball and basketball in grade school
and high school. He was the leading scorer in Chattanooga as a senior in high
school. As a member of the Bombers, a basketball team for another kind of
senior, he says the scoring is more evenly divided.

Two of his team members on the Bombers, Judge Shattuck said, were teammates of his in high school. Another played for rival Tyner High. As much as he
values the physical benefits of basketball, the judge said he puts the most stock
in the congeniality and friendships that have formed among the teammates.

The team of 70- to 74-year-olds has played in the Senior Olympics since 1999,
winning in their age group the last three years. The games are played three-on-
three half-court.

"There's a concession to our age and all," Judge Shattuck said, "no dunking."
But only, he insisted, because the rules don't allow it.

HITTING THE RIGHT NOTES

Rev. Dr.
Virgil Caldwell

The Rev. Dr. Virgil Caldwell started playing the saxophone for the same reason young men do most things.

"Someone told me," he said, "that girls like saxophone players."

Dr. Caldwell cut his musical teeth on the clarinet in high school in Jackson,
Tenn., but later moved on to the sax in college.

He served in the Korean War and taught music for 15 years before joining the
Baptist ministry in 1960.

He recently retired from his 40-year post as minister at New Monumental
Missionary Baptist Church. He hasn't, however, retired from his music or his
writing.

Dr. Caldwell has written about 20 plays, all with religious themes. Years ago,
he said, he cast a man and woman as Joseph and Mary in a Christmas play.
They eventually married.

"I look back on that as one of the most gratifying ..... I've played a ....
ing," Dr. Caldwell said.

As the play brought people together, so too, did the music. Dr. Caldwell's
friend was right. The sax did help him get a girl: his wife, Ruby.

"We've been together for 54 years," he said.

VERB PHOTO BY MARGARET FENTON

Roslynne
Steinberg

PAINTING WITH A PASSION

Roslynne Steinberg is planning to paint pictures of Barack Obama.
"I think there's a call for it," she said.

A native of the Bronx, N.Y., Mrs. Steinberg worked in real estate and
retail. She said she eventually went bankrupt following a divorce. She
came to Chattanooga at 62, moving in with her father and stepmother.
She worked at Belk department store and took oil painting classes at
the Hunter Museum of American Art. She continues to take classes at
Chattanooga State Technical Community College.

Her current painting-in-progress is of a subway platform in Penn Station in New York.

"I always wanted to do a subway station," she said.

Her New York paintings, she said, sell well in Dalton, Ga.

Though she's past the three-quarters of a century mark, Mrs. Steinberg has no plans to slow down. She belongs to Gallery 2 on Main
Street and will be a featured artist in a show in April.

"It's a blessing I discovered I could do this in my 60s," she said. "I
had no idea I could paint."

Cares was a worthy cause along with the Multiple Sclerosis Society and the Siskin Foundation. The Arts for Healing Gala featured my, *China Town NYC* painting. It has been a privilege to have my work embraced by my community and have the opportunity to give back.

As I continued to paint, I was offered many opportunities to display my art. I have had many showings at the Jewish Cultural Center. I was a featured artist at the Mountain City Club in Chattanooga by invitation of my financial advisor, Michael Cartwright. I was nearly eighty years old, never imagining that when I set out to pursue a career in art at sixty-five that I would find myself still painting so many years later.

Health Spring, an HMO, sent out a notice to its members that they were looking for a few inspirational seniors to appear in a television commercial. I was open to the opportunity for a new adventure, so I sent in my application and was thrilled to be chosen. Instead of payment, we were given a trip, all expenses paid, to Portland, Oregon. I felt like it was a royal Hollywood experience. There were professional make-up artists, a wardrobe mistress, lights, and action! We were treated like stars. I had no idea making a commercial could be so much fun, and I was basking in the limelight. The commercial aired for a few months on major television stations. People would stop and ask, "You look familiar; did I see you on TV?"

In 2006, the Hamilton Community Theatre held open auditions looking for forty something performers to be in the world premiere of Paul Fleishman's teen book "Zap." Although I had never set foot on a stage and was seventy-two years old, I was chosen for a part. Once again, tenacity and unwavering belief in myself steadied my course. I knew no matter what happened at this point in my life, I was going to choose me.

I was a member of the Jewish Cultural Center. An opportunity led to a picture I had painted being selected by the Jewish Agency, the largest Jewish Partnership in the world, to

'NITY NEWS   COMMUNITY.TIMESFREEPRESS.COM   • • • Wednesday, January 2, 2008 • Page 9

East Brainerd ARTS

BY BRANDI SCOGGINS
COMMUNITY NEWS WRITER

Hit the Lights!

S ince it first formed in 2005, the Hamilton Community Theatre's mission has been to build relationships with the community. The group services the Brainerd/East Brainerd, Ooltewah and Collegedale areas especially, and as it brings the 2007 season to a close, it continues to seek new members and a permanent venue for the upcoming 2008 lineup.

Hamilton Community Theatre prepares for 2008 season

"We really want to keep going, and what we hope to accomplish with this company is to continue to provide theater performances to the East Brainerd and other local areas on this side of town because there really isn't much out here," explained Rosemary Wallace, producing director of the Hamilton Community Theatre. "We encourage anyone to come out to our open auditions."

Experienced and inexperienced actors alike are welcome, as long as they have a passion for the theater and want to actively take part in building community relationships in fun and different ways. "In fact, many of our cast members for past performances were never on stage before they came and joined us," Ms. Wallace said.

The company strives to produce only family-friendly shows, and also works to keep admission prices low so that entire families can attend and participate in the theater experience. The company's philosophy states that theatre builds neighborhoods and communities by bringing people together to produce enjoyable quality shows for friends and neighbors.

"It's all about relationships, the people and businesses in the community," Ms. Wallace said. "Our goal is to play nice with others and keep the drama on the stage where it belongs."

The Hamilton Community Theatre does not precast any shows, and its audition routines consist of mainly cold readings and a song, when appropriate. The company is now preparing for a new show for the coming spring season, and auditions will be announced this month. Past productions presented by the company include "Zap," based on the hit teen book written by Paul Fleischman, "Jazz A-B-Z," "Searching for Eden: The Diaries of Adam and Eve" and "Children's Letters to God."

E-mail Brandi Scoggins at bscoggins@tfpcommunitynews.com

WHAT'S PLAYING?

Barry Bradford, as King Richard II, delivers a dramatic monologue in the Hamilton Community Theatre's production of "Zap."

Characters Audrey (Roslynne Steinberg) and Irv (Jeffrey Hunter) perform in the world premiere of Paul Fleischman's teen book, "Zap."

From left, Dale Wallace, operations manager, and Rosemary Wallace, production director of the Hamilton Community Theatre, stand with Paul Fleischman, author of "Zap."

Picture in the article above is Roslynne, at age 72, playing a woman aged 40 in "Zap" at the Hamilton Community Theatre

East River and the New York Skyline at Dusk was shown in *The Sound of Many Waters* exhibit at Bible Lands Museum in Jerusalem, Israel

Times Square on New Years Eve

hang in their exhibit. I had painted a picture of the *East River and the New York Skyline at Dusk*. It was on display in the show called *The Sound of Many Waters* at Bible Lands Museum in Jerusalem for a year. The exhibit traveled to Jewish Cultural centers throughout the world and arrived home for the last showing at the Jewish Cultural Center in Chattanooga. This was a highlight of my career.

EAST BRAINERD COMMUNITY NEWS   • • • Wednesday, December 13, 2006 • Page 7

East Brainerd ARTS

New York state of mind

New Yorker Steinberg finds home, second career in Scenic City

BY JENNIFER CATHEY
COMMUNITY NEWS WRITER

Roslynne Steinberg sells some of her paintings at the Raintree Gallery in East Brainerd.

A s a young promoter, Roslynne Steinberg spent time with New York City's bohemian crowd. She liked being around the free-spirited artists that populated the Big Apple. She spent her time arranging art shows and helping artists display their work.

"I had a creative job," she said.

Ms. Steinberg also got involved with real estate in New York City. Her talkative personality and charming demeanor made her suited for working with people. She had an enjoyable, successful life in a city she loved.

Her good luck, however, didn't last.

At the age of 62, bad fortunes in New York caused Ms. Steinberg to make the decision to move south. She could live within her means in the Chattanooga area. The cost of living here is much cheaper than the cost of living in New York.

After her move, Ms. Steinberg began to think up ways to supplement her income. She remembered the artists she saw in New York City and wondered if she had that talent. She thought if she could sell paintings for about $25 each, she would be able to supplement her income.

"I had no idea that I could paint or draw," Ms. Steinberg explained.

When she started painting, Ms. Steinberg knew what she wanted to paint — New York City. Painting has become a way for Ms. Steinberg to reconnect with the city she loves.

"When I paint, I feel like I'm in New York," she said.

Looking at Ms. Steinberg's paintings, it's easy to see exactly why the native New Yorker could get lost in the oil paints, canvases and brushes. It's as easy to get lost in her paintings as it is to get lost in New York.

Ms. Steinberg's almost stylized work seems to jump from the canvas. The colors are cool and funky, and the art itself showcases the artistic feeling of New York City. Crowds roam the city streets. Tourists look up and out at the city's tall buildings. Native

One of the bright, stylistic paintings of New York City Roslynne Steinberg paints. This one is part of her new rain series.

Roslynne Steinberg creates paintings of her native New York City in her studio.
PHOTOS BY JENNIFER CATHEY

A self-portrait by Roslynne Steinberg.

New Yorkers stroll the city streets in long, confident strides. The shade of gray Ms. Steinberg uses on her New York City buildings feels alive.

While Ms. Steinberg enjoys painting the city where she lived for 62 years, she also has some impressive portrait work. She will occasionally paint portraits for people. She realized she has the ability to capture people with her portraits, even if she hasn't met the person she is painting.

"When they (a client) saw the portrait, they cried," she said, adding that it was a great feeling to paint something that moved people so much.

At her first show, Ms. Steinberg said she didn't particularly plan to sell anything. She was allowed to bring one painting and display it. If that painting sold, she would be allowed to bring another.

Ms. Steinberg's first painting sold quickly for a much higher price than the original $25 she envisioned.

So did her second.

"That was when I could call myself an artist," she said.

E-mail Jennifer Cathey at jcathey@tfpcommunitynews.com

More examples of media interest in the artist from New York

Chattanooga Times Free Press

Arts

'From New York City to Chattanooga'

Roslynne Steinberg depicts home in two places

By Ann Nichols
ANNSNICHOLS@AOL.COM

Roslynne Steinberg has translated memories of living in New York City for 62 years, as well as her new home in Chattanooga, onto canvas.

Her solo exhibition of 12 oil paintings, "From New York City to Chattanooga," is on display at Studio 2/Gallery 2 through April 30.

Ms. Steinberg said she colored with crayons as a child, but it wasn't until she was almost 65 years old that she decided to get serious.

"I began taking art classes at the Hunter Museum of American Art, and that is where I met Vicki Daniel White," she said. "She introduced me to oils and encouraged me to study art at Chattanooga State Technical Community College."

For the past 14 years Ms. Steinberg has been attending Michael Holsomback's painting classes there.

Although she misses her native New York, she has many photographs of relatives, neighbors and familiar places from which to paint.

"I add people, places, colors and events from memory, too, and create what I feel," she said.

But, she says, Chattanooga is her home now. It's a city she has "learned to love and paint with passion."

A reception for the show will be held on Friday from 5:30 to 8 p.m. The gallery, 27 W. Main St., is open 10 a.m.-4 p.m. Tuesday through Friday and 11 a.m.-2 p.m. Saturday. For information, call 266-2222.

STAFF PHOTO BY ALLISON KWESELL
Roslynne Steinberg painted "Waiting for the C Train" with oils on canvas.

Page 8 • Wednesday, August 2, 2006 • •   NORTH RIVER

North River ART

She'll take New York

By Cari Gervin
COMMUNITY NEWS WRITER

Roslynne Steinberg never thought she'd be an artist.

Instead, unlike most artists, Ms. Steinberg started painting as a way to make money. Then she fell in love with it.

Ms. Steinberg moved to Chattanooga from Queens, N.Y., in the mid-1990s. She was divorced and bankrupt and had no choice but to move in with her elderly father, even though she herself was in her 60s.

Living on Social Security, selling shoes at Belk, and with just $3,000 left to her name, Ms. Steinberg decided to take up painting, hopeful that she would be able to sell her work and supplement her income.

In 2000, after many classes, Ms. Steinberg sold her first work, a scene of Times Square filled with New Year's Eve revelers.

Since then, her oil snapshots of her native city have continued to fly off the gallery walls. She has been featured in shows at the Association for Visual Artists and the Creative Arts Guild and is about to have her second one-woman show.

Ms. Steinberg, 73, laughs about her younger days,

maybe 30 years ago, when she used to hang out with a group of artists and bohemians in the city.

"I used to envy them. I had no idea I'd be one of them one day," Ms. Steinberg said with amazement.

Despite her decade in Chattanooga, Ms. Steinberg's subject matter remains firmly rooted in her hometown. While she paints portraits of her family and other works on commission, she said she feels compelled to return to New York again and again, even taking several trips a year up north to take photographs (and see her grandchildren).

"I guess I miss New York," Ms. Steinberg sighed. "I love painting it — it puts me into New York."

E-mail Cari Gervin at cgervin@tfpcommunitynews.com

Roslynne Steinberg holds up an unfinished painting of her son, who died from leukemia at the age of six. She said that after painting pictures for friends of family members and pets that had passed away, she was inspired to look inward and paint a memorial work for herself.

PHOTOS BY CARI GERVIN

■ IF YOU GO:
Roslynne Steinberg will have an artist's reception on Friday, Aug. 4, from 5:30 p.m. to 7 p.m. at Gallery 111, 111 W. King St. in downtown Dalton, Ga. Her works will remain on exhibit the rest of the month. For more information or directions, call the gallery at 706-259-4371.

"The Tourists," oil, 2005.

Arts

Transplanted New Yorker Roslynne Steinberg conveys the vibrancy of city life in her art.

Page 7.

tfp **ONLINE.com**

From the play *Zap*, a self portrait of Roslynne and her leading man

FROM NEW YORK CITY TO CHATTANOOGA
Paintings by Roslynne Steinberg

Studio2 / Gallery2
March 20 – April 30

Artist Reception
Friday, March 27
5:30 pm – 8:00 pm

Waiting for the C Train, 2009

ber 10, 2008 • • •   COMMUNITY.TIMESFREEPRESS.COM   HIXSON WEEKLY

Hixson ARTS

A Happy Accident

North River Civic Center showcases paintings by Accidental Auditors

BY KATY MENA
COMMUNITY NEWS ASSISTANT EDITOR

Olga de Klein, Peter Ewing and Roslynne Steinberg, from left, comprise art collective the Accidental Auditors. The group is currently being featured at the North River Civic Center as part of the Visual Arts Exhibition program.
PHOTOS BY KATY MENA

ON DISPLAY

■ The Accidental Auditors exhibit will be on display at the North River Civic Center through the month of October. An opening reception will be held Sept. 28 from 4 to 6 p.m. For more information call 870-8924.

N orth River Civic Center is presenting a new selection of work by local painters known as the Accidental Auditors beginning this month.

Artists Roslynne Steinberg, Olga de Klein and Peter Ewing come from all walks of life. One is a former Realtor from New York City, another an adventurer from Amsterdam. The third is an architect who once called New Jersey home.

The public is invited to a reception to be held at the North River Civic Center Sept. 28 from 4 to 6 p.m.

Though they all met accidentally while auditing art classes at Chattanooga State, their common appreciation for expression and their instructor, Michael Holsomback, has become a driving force behind their creations.

"This is a miracle for me," said Ms. Steinberg. "I feel like I would be old if I hadn't done this. This keeps me going and flowing."

Depicting colorful Manhattan street scenes, Ms. Steinberg's work possesses a vibrant quality that takes the viewer on an urban safari and at the same time awakens the artist herself.

"It's my legacy," said Ms.

Steinberg. "This is my third life." Ms. de Klein was also look-

ing for a certain rebirth when she signed up for Mr. Holsomback's class.

"When I paint I feel more alive," said Ms. de Klein, who has traveled to exotic locales all over the world.

Her global perspective is apparent in her work, which portrays indigenous people from places far and wide.

Similarly, Mr. Ewing's work commemorates individuals from far off places, though his subject matter keeps a distance through time rather than space. His paintings are of family from generations past and possess a nonchalant elegance that he rarely gets to explore in his professional life as an architect.

"Architecture is very precise and very orderly," said Mr. Ewing. "I always feel like I'm sort of looking for little accidents, little expressions."

E-mail Katy Mena at kmena@tfpcommunitynews.com

"Village Happening" by Roslynne Steinberg.

"Runners" by Olga de Klein.

"Here Come the Boomers" by Peter Ewing.

Village Happening at left. Rolynne's New York heritage, color and style revealed in her work seem to appeal greatly to residents of the South.

'The Accidental Auditors

Peter Ewing, Olga de Klein and Roslynne Steinberg are exhibiting at the Creative Arts Guild in Dalton, Ga.

By Ann Nichols
Arts Writer

They finally got the chance to seriously pursue painting.

Peter Ewing, Olga de Klein and Roslynne Steinberg enjoyed making art as children but got sidetracked by life and circumstances. About 10 years ago, however, they all found themselves auditing Michael Holsomback's art classes at Chattanooga State Technical Community College and have continued ever since.

Referring to themselves as "The Accidental Auditors," the three artists approached the Creative Arts Guild in Dalton, Ga., and secured an exhibition of the same name.

On display through Jan. 18, "The Accidental Auditors" is composed of oil paintings that focus primarily on the human figure or face.

Mr. Ewing's large-scale paintings depict individual people, family members or small groups.

"I pick subjects from my collection of photographs or slides that appear to have some story to tell," he said. "I especially like to show the shadows on people's faces while they are engaged in some activity."

Ms. de Klein works from photographs because she said it is difficult for people to pose or sit still for a long period of time. She said she likes to paint portraits because "a face tells a story."

"I am particular attracted to faces of indigent people. Most have endured hardship and have a faith that keeps them going. They are stoic and giving — you can see it in their eyes."

Ms. Steinberg strives to create artworks that tell a story also. Many of them illustrate scenes from her native New York City and her family and friends who still live there. From her large collection of photographs, she chooses one that "strikes her fancy" and begins painting. Often, she incorporates memories from the past into the piece.

The guild, 520 W. Waugh St., is open from 9 a.m. to 6 p.m. Monday through Thursday, 9 a.m. to 4 p.m. on Friday and by appointment. For information, call (706) 278-0168.

Staff Photos by Tim Barber
Capturing the shadows on the faces and figures of his subjects is important to Pete Ewing, who painted "The 70's-SSP."

Olga de Klein, who was born in the Netherlands and has lived in Mexico and South America, enjoys painting portraits because she feels that a face tells a story.

Roslynne Steinberg, a native of New York City, uses her hometown as the inspiration for her oil paintings.

2008 • • •   COMMUNITY.TIMESFREEPRESS.COM   EAST BRAINERD WEEKLY

East Brainerd ARTS

By Brandi Scoggins
Community News Writer

From the Big Apple to the Scenic City

Roslynne Steinberg brings New York flavor to local art lovers

Artist Roslynne Steinberg brings one of her greatest loves to the East Brainerd area through painting. A native of New York for 62 years, she now resides in the Scenic City and currently has her talent on display at the Jewish Cultural Center just off North Terrace.

During her childhood, Ms. Steinberg loved to draw and as an adult she worked as a promoter of shopping malls but never pursued a career in art until after her retirement.

"I would see these senior citizens selling these little paintings and think, 'maybe I'll learn to paint,'" she said.

Following this desire, Ms. Steinberg began taking art classes at Chattanooga State in water color and oil painting. Her first painting that hung in an exhibit sold for $179.

"It just seemed to flow from my brush," Ms. Steinberg said.

From that time, Ms. Steinberg discovered her painting skills were naturally very widely varied. Painting everything from landscapes to portraits, she finds great joy in this activity that she said helps keep her young. However, her native New York still claims some of her time once each year when she visits the city.

"When I paint the scenes of New York, it brings me back into time," explained Ms. Steinberg. "The memories of my life just come back to me and I feel very blessed."

The scenes of New York range from the stock exchange to Ground Zero and everything in between. Ms. Steinberg works from photographs taken on her trips to make sure she captures every detail in her own unique style. She added that the process of painting itself is very special to her and she feels it's miraculous that she can paint each image so well.

"I often finish a painting

ON DISPLAY

■ Roslynne Steinberg will have an exhibit at the Jewish Cultural Center through July 26. Her work will also appear in the new downtown gallery Studio 2 on W. Main Street, which is set to open at the beginning of July.

A native of New York, Roslynne Steinberg now finds herself painting scenes of downtown Chattanooga.

Artist Roslynne Steinberg brings her beloved New York City to Chattanooga through her original oil paintings.

Photos by Brandi Scoggins

and step back and think, 'did I do that?'" she said.

In addition to her paintings of New York, Ms. Steinberg's love of Chattanooga has now made its way into her brushstrokes. She has two recent pieces of local scenes from the downtown Chattanooga area on display at the Jewish Cultural Center.

E-mail Brandi Scoggins at bscoggins@tfpcommunitynews.com

An article in the *Chattanooga Times Free-Press* in July, 2008 features *Rainy Day on Broad*

ARTS
Roslynne Steinberg brings New York flavor to local art lovers.
Page 6.

NORTH RIVER WEEKLY   COMMUNITY.TIMESFREEPRESS.COM   • • • Wednesday, September 24, 2008 • Page 9

North River **ARTS**

"Village Happening" by Roslynne Steinberg.

Olga de Klein, Peter Ewing and North Chattanooga resident Roslynne Steinberg, from left, comprise art collective the Accidental Auditors.

The group is currently being featured at the North River Civic Center as part of the Visual Arts Exhibition program.

PHOTOS BY KATY MENA

Exhibit highlights Roslynne Steinberg

BY KATY MENA
COMMUNITY NEWS ASSISTANT EDITOR

The work of North Chattanooga resident Roslynne Steinberg is currently on display at the North River Civic Center as part of an exhibit created by the Accidental Auditors.

Comprised of Ms. Steinberg and painters Olga de Klein and Peter Ewing, the Auditors is an artistic collective that has given new life to all of the artists involved.

"This is a miracle for me," said Ms. Steinberg, a former Realtor from New York City. "I feel like I would be old if I hadn't done this. This keeps me going and flowing."

Depicting colorful Manhattan street scenes, Ms. Steinberg's work possesses a vibrant quality that takes the viewer on an urban safari and at the same time awakens the artist herself.

"It's my legacy," said Ms. Steinberg. "This is my third life."

Interested parties may view Ms. Steinberg's legacy at the North River Civic Center through the month of October. An opening reception will be held Sept. 28 from 4 to 6 p.m. For more information call 870-8924.

E-mail Katy Mena at kmena@tfpcommunitynews.com

"Runners" by Olga de Klein.

Roslynne's painting *Village Happening* is pictured to the upper left in this article by Katy Mena in the *Chattanooga News Free-Press* in September, 2008. Ms. Mena writes, "Depicting colorful Manhattan street scenes, Ms. Steinberg's work possesses a vibrant quality that takes the viewer on an urban safari and at the same time awakens the artist herself."

Copy of the
original
painting
*Trudg-
ing Times
Square* that
was stolen
from an art
exhibit at
Chattanooga
State in 2007

Copy of the replacement painting, *Trudging Times Square* that was purchased by developer John Wise in 2012

The Daily Citizen   Wednesday, October 4, 2006   **7A**

'Still Doing It,' First Friday to open concurrently

SPECIAL TO THE DAILY
CITIZEN

This Friday marks concurrent openings at the Creative Arts Guild. "Still Doing It" is in the main gallery and shows the work of 16 local and regional artists during three periods of their careers.

In Gallery 11J, relocated this past week to the Guild's main facility, is Atlanta/Austin photographer Bryan Buchanan. Concurrent receptions begin at 5:30 p.m. at the 520 W. Waugh St. facility.

Still Doing It artists are Verina Baxter, Harriet Chipley, Georgia Cress, Ed Kellogg, Mary Britton Lynch, Roslynne Steinberg, Juanita Tumelaire and Alan White from the Chattanooga area; Routh Cline, Marie Stull Crosby, Johnnie Dobson, Barbara Grass, Bernice Spigel and Terry Tomasello from the Northwest Georgia area and Roberta Griffin and Ray Pierotti from the Atlanta area.

The show includes painting, printmaking, sculpture, photography, pen and ink, pottery, mixed media, textiles and works on canvas and paper.

"I like to think of myself as a late bloomer, even though I recently reached the big seven-oh," said artist Roslynne Steinberg.

"For over six decades I lived in New York and moved to Chattanooga in 1994. My life completely changed when I discovered the High Street area and joined the Hunter museum of American Art, where I attended various art workshops, such as painting on silk, watercolor, drawing, and oil painting."

Her studies include class work at Chattanooga State.

Verina Baxter says of her work, "Within hours of my first introduction to sculpting in stone I was hooked. Few art forms or female career options provide the need for such aggressive energy whether manual or mechanical as I use in my initial contact with the stone.

"In contrast there can be a relaxed comfort of file moving against stone in the finishing stages of the process. It is very satisfying to begin with something so hard and crude, and work to release the beauty hidden inside by nature," Ms. Baxter said.

Dalton artist Bernice Spigel has lived a life devoted to both the arts and arts administration.

"It is not easy for me to paint," Ms. Spigel said. "I have 'rituals.' I clean my studio. I arrange my paints. I carefully position my easel and canvas and lights. I check in my

Several artists are participating in Still Doing It, a showing of art by artists over age 50. At left is Barbara Mayo Grass' untitled portrait and is an oil on canvas from 1964. At right is an oil on canvas painted in 2000 by Roslynne Steinberg.

several museums and numerous corporate and private collections.

She has curated 80 major exhibitions as gallery director at KSU, many with catalogs that she researched and wrote.

Born in Anniston, Ala., George A. Cress earned his bachelor of fine arts from Emory University. He served as president of the Tennessee Arts Council and from 1951 to 1984, and was painter in residence at the University of Tennessee at Chattanooga. The Cress Gallery of Art at the University of Tennessee bears his name.

Cress was a member of the faculty of the University of Tennessee at Chattanooga since 1951 and former head of its Department of Art. Now in retirement, Cress remains active in support of the Gallery and its programs and, as Gerry Professor of Art Emeritus, continues to inspire students as he instructs selected courses within the Art curriculum.

Potter Johnnie Dobson earned his bachelor of science in art education from the University of Georgia in 1978. For nine years, he taught two-dimensional and three-dimensional art and art history at Calhoun High School. He and his wife, Penny, are exhibitors at numerous art shows in the southeast. Johnnie teaches drawing, painting, and pottery using free form building of clay slabs. Johnnie also serves as the clay instructor and the facility manager at the Harris Arts Center in Calhoun.

Ed Kellogg developed his artistic interests early studying of Art, the DeCordova Museum School, and, as a member of the Worcester Art Museum School. He has worked in numerous mediums over the past five decades working to develop printmaking and exploration of needlework and textiles.

Mary B. Lynch earned her

education included studying painting three years at Wheaton College in Illinois, after which he transferred to San Diego State University receiving a degree in art in 1966 and a master's in painting and printmaking in 1968. After a year of public school teaching and two years in the Army, Kellogg worked and studied under Dutch Artist Kenk Krüger at Patmos Workshop and Gallery in Toronto, Canada.

In 1973, he took a teaching position at Covenant College on Lookout Mountain in Georgia where he is presently professor of art.

Ray Pierotti was educated in Europe, the Far East and the United States, with degrees in philosophy, language and music.

"I am inclined in my paintings and surface designs to work in a serial manner, exploring a single subject's broad color and structural potential," said Pierotti, adding "Firmly rooted in the material world of wave and particle physics and spiritually inclined towards mysticism, Eastern and Western philosophies are merged into a personal visual language. I am currently driven to abstract designs in landscapes; however, the tenor of my painting is as much a landscape of the soul as that of place. Scenes remembered and scenes invented commingle like the smells, the tastes and the textures of memorable lives."

Juanita Tumelaire is an experienced artist and educator who has studied printmaking at the Massachusetts College

Hopps Merit Award, at the Contemporary Artists Center in North Adams, Mass. She has recently begun creating limiting edition fine art books, and has participated in the Paper and Book Intensive Workshops. At PBI, she learned the structure of the Tibetan Book, which she has adapted for the books she is currently making. She was most recently awarded the Elizabeth Morse Genius Foundation Medal of Honor in Printmaking for her etching "For Raphael Lemkin" in the National Association of Women Artists Exhibit in New York

Terry Tomasello has 23 years of professional arts-related experience. She currently serves as executive director of the Creative Arts Guild, a 43-year-old community-based arts organization serving Northwest Georgia, where she manages the daily operations of a multidisciplinary facility.

Tomasello received her education at the Atlanta College of Art, Georgia State University and The Art Institute of Atlanta. Before moving to Dalton five years ago, she was co-owner and operator of a multi-media firm, Splash Studios, in Atlanta. She is the recipient of the ITVA (International Television and Video Association Award), The Communicator Award and numerous visual arts awards for her photography and sculpture.

Alan White received his master of fine arts in painting from the University of Cincinnati in 1972 and, since that time, has been affiliated with The University of Tennessee at Chattanooga. At UTC, he holds the position of professor of art (and department head emeritus), having served for 20 years as the head of the Department of Art. In 2004, as was his plan after 20 years of administrative responsibilities," he returned to teaching and painting.

Barbara Grass received her education at Vesper George School of Art in Boston Massachusetts. Ms. Grass worked with the ad agency A.W. Ellis and Co. in Boston whose accounts included L.L. Bean. She currently serves as a judge and national instructor for the Embroiders Guild of America where she has won numerous awards for her textile artworks. Ms. Grass has worked in numerous mediums

Chattanooga in 1956. She has done graduate work at the University of Tennessee in Knoxville and Long Island University in New York. Ms. Lynch has been the recipient of numerous awards including the Manhattan Arts Magazine Award of Excellence. She has had well over 40 exhibitions, solo and selected group shows held throughout the United States and in Bombay, Calcutta, China, Moscow, Voronezh, Russia, and New Delhi.

Harriet Chipley is a native of Coral Gables, Fla., and a resident of Lookout Mountain, Tenn. She is a graduate of Duke University with graduate studies in art history at Virginia Commonwealth University, and in art education and painting in UTC and the University of Miami. An arts education for many years and a painter since childhood. She has developed a personal style and point of view through years of work and exposure to different ideas.

Rocky Face artist Routh Cline says of her work "I find that space, order and simplicity of these are driving forces -- they compete with fantasy and imagined scenarios. Disparate elements -- sky, foliage, earth, color, and forms are reshaped and synthesized to form a new whole."

Ms. Cline was included in the recent exhibition Crossing the Threshold with Thelma and Louise held at the Museum of Arts and Sciences in Macon, which was curated by Bernice Steinbaum of the Steinbaum Krauss Gallery in New York City. This exhibition celebrated the strength and resolve of women artists.

Marie Stull Crosby, owner and operator of Color Et Cetera, which specializes in color, styling and design for carpet and rugs as well as digital design and color selection for Chromtact application has journeyed far in the carpet capital of Dalton over the past few decades. Her work has been featured on the cover of New York's Floor Focus magazine and in articles on styling trends and market reports. Clients have included numerous Fortune 500 and 400 companies.

Ms. Stull Crosby is a founding member of the Creative Arts Guild and was the first art chairman. She graduated from Auburn University with a bachelor of applied art and is a native of Birmingham, Ala.

All Creative Arts Guild opening are free and open to the public. For more information please call 706-278-0168 or visit the Guild's Web site at www.creativeartsguild.org

In this article from *The Daily Citizen* featuring several artists' work at different periods in their careers, Roslynne's oil on canvas is pictured on the right. Her comments are in the lead paragraphs to the upper left. She is quoted as saying, "For over six decades, I lived in New York and moved to Chattanooga in 1994. My life completely changed when I discovered the High Street [Art District] area and joined the Hunter Museum of American Art, where I attended various art workshops, such as painting on silk, watercolor, drawing, and oil painting."

On the right, the Twin Towers under construction. On the left, the Twin Towers as they fell on September 11, 2001.

The Twin Towers of the World Trade Center Before 9-11

This painting, *New York Skyline*, hangs in The Big Chill Restaurant in Chattanooga, Tennessee

River Scene, Chattanooga, Tennessee

Rainy Day on Broad in Chattanooga

River Street in Chattanooga

Connections and Losses

It has been amazing how many friends from New York have reappeared in my life in the South. So many fantastic people were part of my life when I needed support, and I will never forget the kindness they showed me when I was down and out. I have tried to return their kindness to others in need. I have built many significant relationships and lasting friendships throughout my life. I am so thankful for the many dear friends that have filled my life with love.

During the period I was going through bankruptcy, I was still in touch with my good friend Rita Albert. She married a kind man named Yussi (Joseph) Seigel. While they were still in Flushing, Queens, I called to see if I could visit. When they opened the door the shock at seeing me, then a haggard shell of my former self, was evident. I had lost so much weight and had thinning hair, a sallow complexion and a missing tooth from recent dental work. I brought them up-to-date on what was happening in my life, and as I left, they pressed a hundred dollars into my hands, insisting I accept it.

Shortly after 9-11 Rita and Yussi moved to Boca Raton, Florida and I was able to visit. At that time, I had regained my health and was doing very well as an artist. I snapped a picture of them hand-in-hand as we were crossing a street to a deli in South Beach. I came home and put it on canvas. It is one of my favorite paintings and made all the more special when I was able to give it to them as a gift. Yussi has since passed away, but I know Rita treasures that painting of the two of them. It is a reminder that they were in love and how much they enjoyed their time together.

In the early 1970s while I was working at the New Rochelle Mall, I befriended a leasing agent named Gilbert Lahn, who was going through a stressful time in life. It's been more than forty years, but we still talk every Sunday morning.

Rita and Yussi Seigel in Boca Raton, Florida

My cousin Howard Luban, Aunt Mae's son, moved to Phoenix, Arizona, with his family. Aunt Mae visited me once in Chattanooga, and I went to see her in Arizona. So many years had passed since we were children in the Bronx at 1320 Manor Avenue. I was thankful for our time together. Aunt Mae died in a nursing home, and I lost my dear cousin Howard in 2013. I promised him I would keep in touch with his wife, Lana, which I gladly do.

Dear Aunt Tess, my early mother figure, has passed away. Her husband, Lester, died shortly after she did. I am happy to have a good relationship with their daughter, Alexis. Uncle Abe, my grandmother's caretaker during so many challenging years, his wife Jean, and their daughter Carole have also said goodbye to this life. I still keep in touch with Abe's son, Norman Jacobs. His two sons will carry on the Jacobs name.

As the years go by, sometimes in a slow canter and sometimes at the speed of light, I am ever more aware of my own mortality. I am grateful for my health, family, friends. I am especially grateful to have discovered the gift of painting at age sixty-five and that I am still able to paint. I am thankful to have laid down my worries, fears and insecurities and look forward to each new day.

My two sons, Stephen and Mark June, 2015

Overflowing Joy

In 2006, on a Saturday night, the day before Mother's Day, I received an unanticipated phone call. It was Mark inviting me to have breakfast for Mother's Day! I was shocked to hear his voice, and when he said, "Would you like to have breakfast on Mother's Day?" It never occurred to me that he was in Tennessee. He said, "I'm in Knoxville and on my way to your house." My heart was overflowing with joy. I had gotten an occasional call on Mother's Day, but never a personal visit. While we were not close, I loved Mark dearly and could not wait to see him.

On his drive from Knoxville to Chattanooga, we talked by cell phone more than we had in years. When he arrived at my place in Chattanooga, we kissed and hugged, and the burden of being estranged from my son lifted from my soul. Mark took me to breakfast at The Back Street Inn, and we walked the Walnut Street Bridge together and then went to lunch together.

Stephen called and said, "Why don't you drive back to New York with Mark?" Mark welcomed the idea. I didn't hesitate to pack my things, and in the blink of an eye, we were off on a seventeen-hour drive. We stopped often to eat and rest, and I was thrilled to become acquainted with an expressive, open part of my son that I had never known.

I stayed with Stephen and Angela and got reacquainted with my grandchildren. Stephen and Angela's two daughters, Alexandra and Elizabeth, had grown into beautiful young women. Mark and Mira's daughters, Lorraine and Sandy, were equally precious. After a joyful ten days, Mark and Stephen bought me a plane ticket home to Chattanooga. There was still much to be resolved, but this had been the best Mother's Day of my life. My family was back. No amount of success, friends, or work could take the place of loved ones. Donald will always hold a treasured place in our family, and he is never forgotten. If I died tomorrow, I would go to my grave happy and fulfilled. Mark returned for a visit on Mother's Day in 2015. I am on cloud nine to have such a joyful relationship with my son.

Mark at the Dead Sea

Stephen's Big Catch

The Stephen Steinberg family in 2015: left to right: Michael Schnupp, Alexandra, Jonathan and Elizabeth Wachter, Angela & Stephen

Left to right, standing: Angela, Stephen, Mark, Lorraine and Lee Eiteberg; seated, Roslynne, Avi and Sandy Weberman, and Mira

The Adventure Continues

My life journey has taken me many places in New York, from the Bronx to Deer Park, Jamaica, Elmhurst, Pearl River, and North Babylon. I spent a short time in North Carolina. I never expected to settle in Eastridge, Tennessee and finally Chattanooga. I realize that living with joy is a choice. No matter the lot we were cast at birth, and no matter how difficult the journey, life is a beautiful gift.

I am nearing my eighty-third birthday as I finish this book, and I am still actively involved in my painting career and still working on various commissions. Many of my paintings are in private homes throughout the country and the world. I have work in New York, Israel, Australia, Brazil, and Italy. Many of my paintings can be seen around Chattanooga. There are two large works transferred onto metal hanging on the outside wall of The Big Chill on Cherokee Boulevard. Others hang in the downtown offices of Raymond James and in the clubhouse at Hayden Place. Many are in private homes.

The broken fences in my family life have been mended, and I have been fortunate to know my grandchildren. Mark's daughter, Lorraine, is married to Lee Eiteberg and they have a daughter named Hayden, my first great-grandchild. Sandy married Rabi Avi Weberman and they plan to have many children. Stephen's daughter, Elizabeth, is married to Jonathan Wachter. Alexandra, Stephen's oldest daughter, is happy with Michael Schnupp. I am blessed with many good friends, some from New York and many from my life in Chattanooga. I am thankful for good health and a sharp mind, laughter and tears, and the comforts and security of my own home.

~ ~ ~

Sometimes I feel as though I have done all the living my mother lost out on when I was born. I still don't know what circumstances caused her mental decline that set the course of so many lives in an unexpected direction.

Over the years, I've had a recurring dream. I have it now at eighty-two. I am back in the tenements at Seabury Place looking for Mother. I don't know which apartment she lives in. They all look alike, grim and featureless brown brick. I search and search until rising like a ghostly apparition, Mother appears in my mind. She is perfectly normal and surrounded by an aura of love as if death freed her as a prisoner of herself.

This is a passing moment of Wishful Thinking.

This painting, *Tribute in Memory of Mama Dora*, will be on display in Israel during 2016 as part of an Israeli-American cooperative exhibit.

Warnock Pro and Birch on LSI 70# white
Design and type by Karen Paul Stone

To order more copies of

Never Having to Say Could Have, Should Have, Would Have

Copy this page, complete information, and mail with check or money order to
**Roslynne Steinberg, 900 Mountain Creek Rd, Box K143
Chattanooga, TN 37405**
-or go to-
www.waldenhouse.com/books -or- your favorite retailer

- -

Name_____

Shipping address _____

City _____ State _____ Zip _____

Phone_____ E-mail(optional for shipping confirmation)_____

    Quantity _____ book(s) @ $18.95   = $ _____
    Shipping first book   = $ ___5.00___
    Shipping quantity _____ additional books @ $3.00 = $ _____
    TN residents add sales tax @ .0925   = $ _____
                      TOTAL = $ _____

- -

Name_____

Shipping address _____

City _____ State _____ Zip _____

Phone_____ E-mail(optional for shipping confirmation)_____

    Quantity _____ book(s) @ $18.95   = $ _____
    Shipping first book   = $ ___5.00___
    Shipping quantity _____ additional books @ $3.00 = $ _____
    TN residents add sales tax @ .0925   = $ _____
                      TOTAL = $ _____

- -

**To Contact the Author
Roslynne Steinberg • ro2art@bellsouth.net
900 Mountain Creek Rd, Box K143, Chattanooga, TN 37405**

CPSIA information can be obtained
at www.ICGtesting.com
Printed in the USA
LVOW05s2316230516

489643LV00046B/1147/P